"I REMEMBER YOU told me, 'No one ever beat Daddy.' "
Amanda looked away as she said, "That's not quite accurate."

"You mean *someone* must have beat him," I asked her.

"*I* did. Once."

"Only once?" I knew I was pushing.

"Only once." She repeated my phrase, and then added, "It was just too great a price to pay."

She squirmed in her chair.

"It's a long story, BarBara, and one I haven't told before, not even to Ted. It's so painful for me. Just the same, I want to tell it. I want to be rid of it. In Texas we used to say, 'Makes no never mind to me,' when we didn't care about something. That has never applied to this. I've cared too much. And way too long. Sometimes, just saying 'Texas' brings it all back."

She took a deep breath to give herself the courage to go on.

"When I think of Texas, I think of the sun, and the way it used to shine on my father. As if it were there just for him.

"My mother had aged. Looking at her, I vowed never to 'let

myself go.' When the Texas sun came out, Mother just looked hot and uncomfortable. She would touch her upper lip and the base of her throat with a lace handkerchief. She would fan herself with whatever was handy, usually the New Testament, and I"—Amanda looked uncomfortable, but forged ahead— "I would be embarrassed for her. In many ways she was a powerful woman, but age had come too early to Mother. It was the one thing she didn't have to wait for.

"But age never seemed to find Daddy. He never seemed to get hot. I felt that Daddy *sought* the sun. Met it straight on. It knew it had met its match."

Amanda's face had been bright, almost mesmerized, and her voice had been animated. Then her tone turned flat.

"That day, at sixteen, I was allowed to shoot skeet with the adults. I had been shooting for years, but always in some sort of junior or girls' group. Now, for the first time, it would be with the adults. With Daddy.

"I had practiced every spare chance I got for that whole summer. It was all that mattered to me. I was consumed with the need to win. When I finally reached the moment of my turn, all I could think of was how much I wanted to please Daddy. How much I wanted to be like him. For him. I remembered everything he had taught me over the long tiresome practice shoots.

"I had the concentration down so well that everything else faded from my mind but the flying disks and the squeeze of the trigger. I swear I didn't hear a sound, wasn't aware of anyone around me, had nothing on my mind other than hitting those disks as they came arcing into my vision. I was so caught up in the moment that it was all over before I fully realized what had happened. Suddenly, there was so much noise and commotion. I had won the shoot. My brothers were jumping up and down and then running toward me. My mother was crying. Daddy was standing off to one side, looking golden. But he was very still.

"They gave me a trophy." Amanda laughed, and broke the

tension for a brief moment. "It was 1968, a good year for trophies in Texas. It was part of Frontier Days and the celebration of the founding of our little town. Daddy had grown a beautiful golden beard as part of the Frontier Days festivities. Just the beard I would have expected from him. But he didn't win a trophy for it. And he didn't win a trophy for skeet shooting. I did."

Amanda paused a moment to regain her composure, which she may have been on the verge of losing. In that moment I reflected on how many stories like this I had heard—how many more I would undoubtedly hear.

I reflected on my growing awareness that women who could come to terms with these old messages could conquer them, while others were still doomed to commit Power Failure.

"On the way home we had to drive past the Big Boy. It was the restaurant where I first ordered something other than a hamburger, where I first ordered something closer to an adult dinner. We never failed to stop there for dinner after shooting at the skeet range. And I never failed to get the jumbo shrimp dinner, with extra sauce on the side. The process of dipping the shrimp was as important to me as the meal itself. When I realized Daddy wasn't slowing down, I couldn't believe it. 'Daddy. Daddy, we're going to pass the Big Boy.'

" 'I'm not hungry,' he said. 'I have things I have to do at home.'

"I started to protest, but my mother put her index finger to her lips and almost imperceptibly shook her head from side to side. Mother was the peacemaker in our family.

"We ate dinner at home that night. It wasn't shrimp. And Daddy didn't have any. He was busy in the garage. Much later, when everyone should have been asleep, I heard him come upstairs. I knew he would have to pass my bedroom on the way to theirs. I had been lying awake, waiting for that moment.

" 'Daddy?' I called to him. There was no answer.

" 'Daddy?' I said it a little louder.

"He said, 'What do you want, Amanda?'

" 'A kiss good night. You always kiss me good night.' I'll never get over what he said then.

" 'Kiss your trophy.' "

POWER
FAILURE

POWER FAILURE

■

Why Women Said "No" to Top
Management Positions—Six Inside
Stories to Help Others Say "Yes"

BARBARA BOOLS

AND LYDIA SWAN

Special Consultant: Dr. Julia Targ

■

St. Martin's Press / New York

Grateful acknowledgment is made for permission to reprint from the following: Terrence Deal and Allan Kennedy, *Corporate Culture,* © 1982, Addison-Wesley Publishing Co., Inc., Reading, Massachusetts. Reprinted with permission. Excerpt from *Women Like Us,* © 1985 by Liz Roman Gallese, used by permission of William Morrow and Company, Inc. Morrison/White/Van Velsor, *Breaking the Glass Ceiling,* © 1987, Addison-Wesley Publishing Co., Inc., Reading, Massachusetts. Reprinted with permission. Excerpt from *Management and Machiavelli* by Antony Joy, used by permission of Holt, Rinehart, and Winston, Inc. Excerpt from *You Can Negotiate Anything,* © 1980, by Herb Cohen, used by permission of Lyle Stuart, Inc. Excerpts from *The Road Less Traveled,* © 1980, and *The Different Drum,* © 1987, by M. Scott Peck, used by permission of Touchstone Books, a division of Simon & Schuster, Inc. Excerpt from *The Cinderella Complex,* © 1981, by Collette Dowling, used by permission of Summit Books; a division of Simon & Schuster, Inc. Excerpts from *Intimate Partners,* © 1987, and *Unfinished Business,* © 1986, by Maggie Scarf, used by permission of Random House, Inc. Excerpts from *Breaking into the Boardroom,* © 1988, by Jinx Melia used by permission of G.P. Putnam's Sons. Excerpts from *Men Who Hate Women and the Women Who Love Them,* © 1987, by Susan Forward and Joan Torres used by permission of Bantam Books, a division of Bantam, Doubleday, Dell Publishing Group, Inc. Excerpts from *The Third Wave,* © 1980 by Alvin Toffler, used by permission of William Morrow and Company, Inc. Excerpts from *The Third Sex,* © 1986 by Patricia McBroom, used by permission of William Morrow and Company, Inc. Excerpts from *Blue Rise,* © 1983 by Rebecca Hill, used by permission of William Morrow and Company, Inc. Excerpt from *Toward a New Psychology of Women,* © 1976 by Jean Baker Miller, used by permission of Beacon Press. Excerpt from *The Myth of Two Minds,* © 1987, by Beryl Lieff Benderly, used by permission of Doubleday, a division of Bantam, Doubleday, Dell Publishing Group, Inc. Excerpts from *Light of the Home,* © 1984, by Harvey Green and Mary E. Perry, used by permission of Pantheon Books.

Design by Guenet Abraham

Library of Congress Cataloging-in-Publication Data

   Bools, BarBara.
     Power failure.
      1. Women—Employment—Psychological aspects.
2. Success. 3. Women executives—Psychology.
I. Swan, Lydia. II. Title.
HD6053.B7333 1989   658.4'09'088042   88-29832
ISBN 0-312-02632-3

First Edition
10 9 8 7 6 5 4 3 2 1

CONTENTS

∎

NOTE TO THE READER

■

THIS BOOK includes some very personal experiences that the men and women herein have shared with me. Sometimes I witnessed and was an integral part of the circumstances. On other occasions the insights and candor were offered by the individuals. As tempting as it might be to speculate as to their identities, the very purpose of this book is to discover and respect their hard-won truths, not invade their private lives to do so. Consequently, to protect their privacy—confidentiality is the very hallmark of our business philosophy—names, descriptions, logistics, and situations have been altered without obscuring the essential substantive realities of the men and women whose lives contributed to this book. I hold them in the deepest regard and respect their struggles to uncover their individual truths.

—BARBARA BOOLS

ACKNOWLEDGMENTS

■

W E FIRST want to thank our husbands, Ron Bools and Ed Jackson. Ron, himself a writer, worked enthusiastically and diligently with great reserves of humor and sensitivity throughout the creation of this book. Ed was always there when we needed him, which was often. His understanding and support and many late-night dinners pulled us all through.

Next, we want to express our deepest appreciation to Julia Targ, Doctor of Clinical Psychology, who along with her private psychotherapy and consulting practice conducts courses in life span development and gender differences. Her expertise in working with the problems of creative people and her understanding of the issues affecting job performance have been invaluable to us in assessing the development of our ideas. Julia's adherence to a strict discipline in examining the text, along with her intelligence and warmth, added a richness to the project.

Our agent, Evan Marshall, confided in us that even if we hadn't elected to have him represent us he still wanted to ensure the proposal ". . . got to someone who would guarantee it would be published." For this early and unflagging support, we can't thank him enough.

Evan brought our proposal to the attention of Toni Lopopolo, executive editor at St. Martin's Press. Toni guided us from proposal to final manuscript with a keen instinct for recognizing and protecting what we wanted to say. This is an amazing skill. We want to thank Toni and her assistants, Robin Kessler and Stacia Friedman, for their trust in us and the recognition that this work represents the expression of a message that is important to all of us.

We especially want to thank our community of partners at Bools & Associates. They pitched in, gave of themselves, and often went the extra mile so this work could come to fruition.

POWER
FAILURE

AMANDA KITCHEN

■

She had it all.
They offered her more.

As AMANDA Kitchen laced through the tables on her way to the podium, I marveled at how appropriately her name fit her: The exotic "Amanda" so keenly represented her outward characteristics, her beauty, her very stately bearing, while "Kitchen" was such a true, plain word that captured her sense of the ordinary, her rootedness. Amanda Kitchen was sophisticated *and* down-home, and thrived on the synthesis of this dichotomy as she approached the man presenting her with advertising's highest honor, bestowed by her peers: the coveted Clio.

In the movie industry, Oscars are awarded to actors who often disappear from the scene not too long afterward, which has led to the "Oscar jinx" theory. In television, dozens of Emmys have been awarded to performers and shows that have already been canceled. But in the advertising profession, when the Clios are handed out, it is almost always to practicing professionals who might have worked late that very day. These are people who are at the very peak of their performance.

AMANDA'S MOMENT

Amanda reached the podium and the warm glow of the spotlight awaiting her, and was handed her Clio statuette by the legendary Howard Roth. As Howard handed Amanda the shiny statue, he did something remarkably out of character for him. He stepped out of the spotlight and relinquished it to that night's golden girl and *her* golden girl.

The crowd went wild. All night there had been genuine applause for the deserving, but it had appeared in pockets of vested interests. There had been nothing that evening that united the crowd like Amanda's win. They were on their feet now, something that had not happened before. And they were shouting. Suddenly, there were no factions, no rivalries, no company tables in the room. Just joy. The kind of joy when something really good happens. And, indeed, something really good was happening in that spotlight.

That something really good was Amanda Kitchen.

Amanda held the Clio close to her heart. She seemed to scan the audience for a face in the crowd. The screen behind her filled with the images of her Clio-winning television commercial, called simply enough, *End of the Day.*

> The camera discovers and follows one mailman at the end of his day who seems to be, if not limping, at least favoring one foot. He lives in a three-story walkup and the camera follows his ascent. There, in his sparse but adequate apartment, he removes his shoes and places shoe trees in them. Then, sitting on the side of the tub, he washes his feet, carefully and gently, patting them dry. Only then does he go to the refrigerator and remove a bottle of beer which he places on the kitchen table as he sits down to look out the window at the street below. As the street sounds grow louder, the camera pans to the bottle

and moves in tightly to its label. Finally, the famous voice (made all the more famous through repeated and exclusive appearances in these commercials) says, "Come share the taste that only experience can provide." It wasn't even necessary to say the product's name—the blue and white and gold label could not, would not, be mistaken. The camera then turns again toward the open window and pans down to two cars on the street below where several people, still in their postal uniforms, pile out in a comfortable, good-natured way, look up to the window, and head toward the building. The theme music swells, and the commercial ends abruptly.

This was Amanda's moment.

CLOSER TO THE TRUTH

I remembered vividly Amanda's story about the genesis of this soon-to-be-legendary commercial. She had fought hard for that spot and won. When she first showed the storyboard of her commercial to the account group at her agency and said she wanted to honor the workingmen and workingwomen of this country, she was met with stony silence. But not for long. Soon her detractors found their voices.

"For Christ's sake. A mailman?"

"Mailmen *shoot* people. You can't blame them after all that junk mail, but Oklahoma's an important market. Do we want to remind those people?"

"Does he have to wash his feet? You can't show feet in a beer commercial. The feet will have to go."

"Is he all alone? Where's Mrs. Mailman? Is he divorced? A widower? Oh, God, Amanda—people will think he's gay. This is the most depressing spot I've ever seen."

"He can't drink alone. It'll look like we're promoting lonely old drunks."

"No feet. Feet are out of the question."

"Couldn't he have a girlfriend? At least a macho guy friend? A dog?"

"I'm taking a stand on feet."

Amanda took her stand too. When it came to the work, she displayed strong, independent values and creative integrity. She believed that her value to the client, to the industry, to the public, was to present products with intelligence and warmth. She did *not* believe that her value lay in pleasing everyone at the agency.

She insisted on presenting the commercial to the client just as it was. She knew if she could get that one through, the others in the campaign would be a snap. She would show respect to all those people who really work for a living, rather than just the ones who populate television commercials. She wasn't talking about models, but real people. Amanda had done her homework. She knew backward and forward the figures and percentages of how much beer was consumed. By whom. Under what circumstances. She also knew her clients at the brewery knew them even better than she did. She believed that if she could get her idea in front of the client, it stood a chance of being seen for what it was: a simple message about a real person. She would fight for that, always; counting on getting something closer to the truth in her commercials than is usually seen.

HER OWN AGENDA

It worked. Sure, she had been forced to add the last bit with the other postal workers. But she had always expected to have to succumb on that point. In truth, she strategically had left it out of the original board so she could go through the requisite paces of "compromising" and "submitting." In her ongoing quest for "more real" advertising, Amanda had schooled herself in presentation skills and negotiating maneuvers. She had learned how to lose the battle gracefully and still undisputably win the war.

Some women enter business thinking that things will go their way if only they work hard and are trustworthy and straightforward. I have seen women behave in a ten-person meeting as they would behave in a family conference—listening to everyone's concerns, trying to solve each stated problem as it comes up, compromising, cajoling, and mediating anger between parties. Acting as though the happiness and satisfaction of everyone in the room were the goal.

Not so with Amanda. She knew that every person in a business meeting had a different agenda, and that most of them were hidden. She considered what every person there would attempt to negotiate for. In stating her suggestions, she started with more than she needed so she would have room to concede a point or two and not actually lose ground. She managed to keep meetings on her own agenda. And she navigated these politics in a disarmingly soft-spoken and charming manner. She was a skilled game player.

SOMEONE I WANTED TO MEET

The last image of the television commercial faded and the spotlight once again found Amanda standing tall and proud in its glow, which only enhanced her own.

I looked over the room. It suddenly had grown hushed to hear the words of the newly acclaimed legend. A few tables over I spotted Lynn Taylor, a business colleague whom I respected and had known for years. We smiled at each other over our shared secret. Lynn made sure my eyes were on her as she carefully formed the words, "I told you so." We both laughed. Indeed, she had.

Several years earlier, Lynn Taylor had suggested I meet Amanda Kitchen. Her exact words had been, "She's the best thing to happen to Manhattan in a long time. She's bright, ambitious, attractive, and funny, funny, funny."

A MENTOR

At that time, several years before her Clio win, Amanda was working at Jones & Livingston (J&L) in Tony Fortuna's group and appeared to be a rather well-kept secret. Tony Fortuna had recently been hired by J&L from a medium-size agency in Dallas, where he was a creative director. He had built his excellent reputation on attracting and developing superb juniors who worked for him. It was my opinion that Tony was not very creative himself but continued to rise on the considerable talents of those he so carefully hired. In my business, I often see careers grow or sour specifically because of a talent—or lack of talent—in hiring. I only wished there were more people in the business—like Tony—who recognized people with superior creative abilities and then had the good sense to get out of their way. This, Tony seemed to do better than anybody. As part of this process, when he accepted the position at J&L, his negotiations included bringing Amanda Kitchen with him. He came in as a creative director. She came in as a copywriter, which is what she had been in Dallas. They both appeared more than satisfied with the continuity of the relationship and Amanda continued to make Tony look good. Very good.

Tony had hired Amanda right out of college. She had come into the agency in Dallas and refused to leave before she had seen him and shown him her work—work that was crude and unsophisticated, with little knowledge of marketing or even the marketplace, but nevertheless had a rough, zany brilliance about it. Tony was very aware of his burgeoning reputation as a mentor and saw Amanda as a real feather—if not *the* feather—in his cap. Amanda, bright and personable, had grown up in a large family of five children, where she was the only daughter. She once laughingly told me that in Dallas she had been only too happy to accept the role thrust upon her of the favorite child with the greatest promise.

AN INDUSTRY HEROINE

It was to be a while before I actually met Amanda, but after the glowing review from Lynn Taylor, I had called to introduce myself.

"Amanda? This is BarBara Bools."

Amanda clearly knew of our consulting and executive search work. "BarBara Bools! Tony Fortuna once told me I'd know when I'd arrived because I'd get a call from BarBara Bools."

I laughed with her, and proceeded to get to know her, over the phone. During this first conversation, she made her agenda clear to me.

"I want to have an influence on this business. This is important work I do, and I want to be important, too, to have the largest reach possible. It might sound harsh, but I'm after power. I want the power to affect change."

At that time I truly believed Amanda was in an excellent position in her career: J&L had a few clients who were open to her type of work, and Tony Fortuna was a strong mentor. I told Amanda that perhaps, one day, one of my clients would have a top executive need that would be her opportunity.

"BarBara, I really mean it—I want the authority to have a grand-scale influence. I'll be ready," Amanda finished.

For the next few years I kept a particularly interested eye

on her, professionally. She was becoming a bit of a heroine in the industry. She proved that products could be advertised with humor and warmth—even intelligence. One of her co-workers told me, "She sells soap with music and heart. Her work is commercial poetry." The trade magazines loved her. She was interviewed and profiled. Her work was featured. The awards started rolling in. She was creating terrific advertising. And she was gaining power.

PROMOTED

Then Tony Fortuna was promoted to group creative director. He quickly offered Amanda a position as an associate creative director in one of his groups. Six months later her work was responsible for landing a major piece of packaged-goods business long coveted by J&L. She was made a full creative director, and while still reporting to Tony Fortuna, Amanda now was directly responsible for a soft drink account with huge billings and dramatic visibility. Best yet, the account was in trouble.

CEMENTING A REPUTATION

Slipping brands are often embraced by talented risk-takers. There's no better way to cement a reputation in advertising or marketing than to turn around a failing brand. (Think about Lee Iacocca—"Mr. Turnaround.")

Success can mean large-scale recognition and rewards. Failure can mean the loss of the account, and possibly even the loss of one's position.

But not the loss of one's reputation. If the challenge turns out to be insurmountable, this is often easily forgiven or explained. It was too late—too much harm had been done by the previous campaign. Salvage efforts were undertaken after too many competitors had a foothold. Consumer trust was irrevocably tarnished. For these reasons, an unsuccessful turnaround artist is still perceived as a bit courageous, and may be given a chance to try again. It can be a risky situation where even failure is understood.

But Amanda felt no need for such a safety net of explanations. She had more self-confidence than most, and absolutely no thought of failure. Like Babe Ruth pointing to where he would hit his next home run, Amanda announced (in an interview—she was possessed of a sense of drama) just exactly when she expected a turnaround in the fortunes of the company and the soft drink product for which she had gained advertising responsibilities. It was a risky statement, made with a confidence that some called foolishness. But she believed in the product, and believed that she could talk to consumers. Amanda's prophecy came true.

Amanda was richly rewarded for this performance, as was her mentor, Tony Fortuna, who had backed her efforts all the way. Tony was promoted from group creative director of J&L's New York office to executive creative director of J&L's Dallas office, a major step up for him, as well as a triumphant return home. Amanda was immediately given the vacancy Tony created. She was now one of only three group creative directors at J&L, and the only woman vice-president at the agency.

In an industry where "a minute here and a minute there" is all that matters—providing a minute here is on "The Cosby Show" and a minute there is on "The Super Bowl"— Amanda's time had come.

∙ ∙ ∙

SEEING THE FUTURE

It was also the time one of our top clients, Bailey/Brumman/ Lancaster Worldwide, involved me in their master plan. B/B/L was one of the top twenty agencies worldwide and boasted a client list of solid, growing international marketing giants, but they had an eye to the future. Video rentals, cable television (examples of the demassification of the media), and greater numbers of working women all meant that consumers were becoming increasingly difficult to get to—and get through to on network television. B/B/L had long been known for good, dependable, workable advertising—fine during an era when every home had two TVs and only three networks. During those decades you could motivate consumers just by running a commercial often enough.

But B/B/L saw the future. Only the rare and wonderful commercials would command attention, keep a viewer from flipping to MTV during commercial breaks. B/B/L wanted to consistently produce advertising that would be remembered if seen only once. A tall order, and one whose time had come.

The agency had plans to restructure in an enlightened way—using people as the cornerstone of their success. The emphasis on people first was twofold: to attract, motivate, and satisfy the very best admakers with already established or growing reputations, and then believe in them, support them. By applying the same attitude toward consumers—attract, motivate, and satisfy them—the agency would have great advertising. The money would follow as a natural result of this focus. This new direction was being planned at a time when many of the giants of the industry viewed their advertising as just another by-product of their vast moneymaking machine. Money was not B/B/L's first objective here. The two-year-old merger and the loyalty of a handful of huge and secure clients put them in a very nice position financially. They could afford to take the high road, to reposition themselves publicly as liberated, enlightened, and humanistic—fully representative of the information-age concepts in our society.

Bools & Associates had worked with Bailey/Brumman/Lancaster for several years. We had had retainers with three of their autonomously operated offices prior to the merger.

AN EXCELLENT CEO

During the merger two years previously, one man had emerged who seemed best able to handle the difficult task of uniting the many factions and branch offices. Essentially, Cliff Eagleton was awarded the position of CEO of B/B/L because "no one hates him." I had known him since he had been promoted to the presidency of one of their branch offices. He was extremely effective, and well liked. Cliff carefully selected his advisors and listened to them. Bools & Associates was one of them.

Cliff had known that the only way to win in a political and divided arena was to be staunchly apolitical and be a good helmsman known for a commitment to the *whole.*

The strategy worked.

The board members had picked Cliff to be CEO of the corporation at a time when a single leader—and unifier—had been crucial to their growth. He was reported to be a unanimous selection, and may have been.

Their selection was sound—he was also an excellent CEO.

■   ■   ■

UPGRADING LEADERSHIP

Bools & Associates had placed most of Cliff's lieutenants—people who reported directly to him and were in place to succeed him—while he headed the branch office. In fact, we had done such a good job in making the matches that there had been only sporadic high-level assignments from Cliff for two years. Now, during the reconstructive merger months, it was time for us to recruit heavily for Cliff again. He wanted help in finding some of the brightest and most innovative people in the industry, people who would work with him to revitalize the company. Everything was in place to upgrade the agency's leadership, and several plum assignments were awarded to our company all at once. Let me tell you about the one that was to involve Amanda Kitchen—the position of executive creative director of their Los Angeles office. This was one of the more visible offices in the system, with show-case accounts, some of which were being mishandled and on the verge of being lost. Turning that office into a creative mecca would point the company in a new direction.

Our company researched the market for unique and quali-fied candidates. Amanda Kitchen's name surfaced from more than one source. Even though she was very young, she was very much a fit, and would make a visible statement. She had been made group creative director a year and a half earlier, and her candidacy made more sense all the time. Though I still hadn't met Amanda face to face, that soon would change.

WORKING HALF DAYS

She answered my call herself, and started by saying she was very happy to hear from me. She mentioned that I had been lucky to reach her, as she was working only half days at present. She told me that she and Ted had a six-month-old baby girl at home. Amanda had convinced Jones & Livingston to allow her to work half days for a while. They had graciously agreed—at half salary.

(I have seen this dozens of times: Even when responsibilities remain the same, a frequent corporate response to half days in the office is half salary, perhaps because management knows the woman has few options. Usually, the woman's reaction includes feelings of hurt, anger, and rejection as well as gratitude and loyalty.)

A SUPPORT ROLE

I detected a slight note of dissatisfaction in Amanda's voice as she spoke about the situation. She had risen to group creative director and a salary of $150,000 with a guaranteed bonus of $20,000, plus good profit-sharing, four weeks vacation, and all the other perks that agencies can and do provide for their stars. But now she was only a part-time writer and troubleshooter for J&L. Sure, she was in on all the new business pitches, but in a support role. The previous year she had spearheaded the new business hit team and could pick and choose from every resource J&L possessed, including their brightest creative talents. But when she left on maternity leave, her group had been disbanded and distributed among other groups. The same had happened to her accounts. Now she was just a resource herself, waiting to be chosen.

NOT WHY SHE WAS HIRED

She paused at this point in her open and easygoing narrative. I sensed a confusion, a thinking-through.

"So your situation now, at J&L . . . ?" I prompted.

"Has changed totally!" She finished the sentence. "I mean, I love this agency. They have been totally supportive of my new motherhood. Lots of time off during delivery and all, and the half-days arrangement was no problem. My house was even full of flowers when I got home from the hospital. But . . ." Again, Amanda paused.

"But?" I asked gently.

"Somehow I'm not a creative director anymore. As I told you before, I want to get to a position of influence. But during the changeover to half time, my group and my accounts were all reassigned, and I was home only a month." She was very much the professional, but growing ever slightly agitated. "Now I'm functioning as a writer with a group creative director title. That's not why Tony hired me! He even told me that he detected real management ability in me early on. BarBara, I can write, but more than that I can *communicate with people.* I know how to motivate and satisfy my staff and clients as well as consumers, and now all that part of my job is gone."

"Amanda, when do you plan to return to work full-time?"

"Within a couple of weeks."

"How will that change your status at J&L?"

She went on to tell me that she would have to struggle again to rebuild a group, to regain not only accounts but credibility. She sounded frustrated with J&L's current management.

"Tony Fortuna was a great boss. If he had still been here during this time, *he* would have known that half days at the office wouldn't mean my mind would shut off the rest of the time. He was always open to innovative ways of living and working. But the top brass here is just very concerned that our clients feel their accounts are, quote—manned one hundred and ten percent—unquote."

She had reason to believe that even as supportive as J&L had been, they would now think of her as only a semi-serious player.

■ ■ ■

AN OPPORTUNITY

It seemed like a good time to consider Amanda for a new opportunity.

She had said she could "motivate and satisfy," echoing almost exactly the new B/B/L credo of Attract, Motivate, and Satisfy. This suggested to me that their philosophies might be compatible. I made a note to explore this further with Amanda.

AN ENLIGHTENED COUPLE

Amanda's husband, Ted Spencer, had been an art director on retail accounts. He had been hired at Jones & Livingston just two months before Amanda started. He worked in their sales promotion section, where his genius for brochure and direct-mail design was the talk of the agency. But this kind of work isn't as visible as television advertising—it's mailed away or given away and eventually thrown away. Amanda's work was on TV. All the networks. Every night.

I wondered how this affected their relationship. Given that they had met at the agency, these differences in their public status had been true *before* they married. Because it is still true that most men marry women somewhat less successful than they are, I was intrigued with the possibility of encountering an enlightened, noncompetitive couple.

MEETING AMANDA

I needed to get to know Amanda better before presenting her with what promised to be the career opportunity of a lifetime.

I wanted to see if she indeed *was* a serious long-term player. If our meeting progressed as I anticipated, I would next ask to meet her spouse, something I frequently do when relocation is involved. (All too often the spouse disrupts the proceedings at the last minute because he or she wasn't included sooner in the decision-making process. Besides, I have never believed it is—or should be—just one person's decision.)

When she came through the door I was a little surprised. Amanda didn't look at all as she had at the Clio banquet. She was smaller in person than I remembered. She was also very casual, wearing nice but indifferently assembled clothes. She wore too much makeup carelessly applied, and carried a huge golf umbrella, which could have been chic with the right outfit and on the right person but managed that day just to seem outsized and make Amanda look clumsy. I wondered about this presentation of herself and what it might say about her self-confidence and sense of proportion. Maybe she didn't feel all that good about herself. Then I smiled inwardly, remembering she was a woman with a six-month-old baby at home. Matched accessories were probably not a priority. Then she spoke and I forgot all about appearances.

Amanda had a captivating, make that *mesmerizing,* voice. She spoke very softly and slowly and I found myself leaning forward in my chair so as not to miss a word. (This is a tactic I've seen used to control the listener's attention.) I was pleased to be in her company and hear her speak. This was a woman who loved the business for what it is—all of it—the game, the product, the chance to express human values and make a lot of money all at the same time. I understood instinctively why clients were enchanted with her and by her.

■　■　■

A PERSONAL QUEST

We discussed her life and her professional goals. Her goals were high—she wanted to reach the very top.

"I am a natural leader," she said. "People get involved in things I get excited about."

More than that, her point of view about advertising shone through as a personal quest. She wanted to show real people, to humanize marketing, to talk to consumers with wit and intelligence. She abhorred stereotypical "women in the kitchen" commercials and felt the need to talk to a broader range of consumers. She liked car commercials aimed at women, detergent commercials at teenagers, mayonnaise spots at men. Her daughter, she said, was being raised by two *people,* not two stereotypes. She wanted to make sure what she saw on TV was as fair-minded. She wanted to talk to *people,* not roles. She wanted to reach the top to have as much influence as possible toward making these things happen.

I liked her. A lot.

THE STRATEGIST IN HER

We talked about her marriage, her happy childhood. I learned she had four brothers, and they had all played together, straightforwardly and honestly. I wondered what effect that had on her relationship with Ted.

"I could beat Mark at kick-the-can, and run faster than Lloyd and ride bareback, which Tom never mastered. It always made Mother nervous but Daddy loved it. John could run faster than I could, but I always beat him at softball. Chess was truly my strong point, though. I still regularly beat Ted at chess."

Yes, I could see the strategist in her, beneath her current casual demeanor. "Did you beat *all* your family?" I asked.

She smiled. "Well, almost. No one ever beat Daddy."

I smiled back. It seemed that the woman had confidence *and* humility.

We spent the rest of the morning—actually much more time than either of us had originally allotted—talking about her agenda. She shared a lot of personal desires, even down to the cities she would consider, L.A. being at the top of the list. I decided to offer her a chance at the B/B/L position. She was intrigued: with the position, the clients, the needs of the agency, the chance to make her mark, the problems (which only *challenged* her—she had built her reputation on turning accounts around), Los Angeles itself. Mostly she was intrigued by the opportunity for power. She wanted very much to pursue this. Ted would love it for both of them, she assured me.

My initial list of fifty-three candidates narrowed, finally, to four. Amanda was far and away the youngest. And the only woman.

Amanda's competition was fierce. The first man headed an agency in Minneapolis that had been winning awards. The second was from another major agency in New York. (And while I knew he wanted this job tremendously, his New York street smarts forbade any show of interest. Some New Yorkers call this "the attitude." It was a case of protesting too much. When confronted, he acknowledged his interest and opened up.) The third male candidate was highly sought after because of his outstanding and effective campaigns.

A NATIONAL TREASURE

Cliff Eagleton arrived with Bob Johnson for a full day of interviews. Cliff was promoting Bob to the presidency of the L.A. office. I had known Bob for years, and thought him an excellent choice. Bob joked with me that he was thrilled to be returning to California after years of living in Connecticut. "Surf is never up in Connecticut, BarBara," he had told me just a month before. "My wife's getting hostile. The dog is morose."

Part of my consulting work with Cliff was to help him identify—from an objective and international viewpoint—the future leaders already within B/B/L who might otherwise be overlooked and lost in the restructuring. So when Cliff Eagleton first confided in me his plans as CEO, I had shared my knowledge with him regarding Bob Johnson.

Bob was now about to be president of the Los Angeles office and was here with Cliff to pick the executive creative director. The three of us were like kids who were finally permitted inside the candy store. There's nothing more exciting than building and creating something fine. The sense of this was everywhere in the room.

SERIOUS CONTENDERS

I briefed them on all four candidates. The three men were undeniably qualified and we discussed them at length. Amanda represented a bit of a risk: she was so young, so unproven as a leader and, yet ultimately, very exciting. Though Bob had never met Amanda, he had seen her and her work at the Clio awards. Amanda was my favorite, but I did not reveal it at this time.

Bob knew the man from New York and laughed out loud when he saw his name on the presentation folder. "I hate that asshole from the last agency" was his pithy comment. After that, when we would mention that individual all Bob could do was refer again to "the asshole." In exasperation I finally said, "Can't you call him anything else?" To which he replied, "All right, he's a *pompous* asshole." I convinced Bob that one unfortunate incident, which the candidate had revealed to me, was not reason enough to eliminate him. His work was exciting and his management skills were proven. Clients loved him and he was responsible for a lot of new business—and he had said he would love to work with Bob.

Going in, there were three serious contenders. And the "pompous one."

MEETING AMANDA

Before Amanda arrived, Bob was reviewing the potential downside of hiring Amanda Kitchen. Struck with the enormity of the task facing the new executive creative director, Amanda began to sound too young, too vulnerable, and maybe too good to be true.

"BarBara. Do you think she'll have managerial strengths?" He didn't wait for an answer. Of course I had discussed all of this with Cliff, but Bob was new to the scene and needed a little catch-up time. "A commanding presence? You know clients have to feel comfortable with someone they're about to hand millions of dollars of business over to. They have to feel confident."

My assistant, Susan, came to the door of the conference room and announced Amanda Kitchen. Bob's fears disappeared within minutes. She was a professional dynamo. This was not the Amanda who had sat in a heap two weeks earlier. This was the new model: sleeker, shinier, loaded with options. Everything was in place and functioning at full throttle. Her brains, her style, her command of the situation, were a thrill to behold. Then there was the added element, one that had decidedly not been present before: The lady was sexy. Very polished, very professional, very much a communicator. Amanda was playing to her audience, and I was delighted to see how she rose to the occasion.

There was a clear electricity in the room. Amanda presented her cassette of television commercials and portfolio, discussed her reasons for being in advertising, her desire to promote products with warmth and intelligence. She said it all with her mesmerizing voice. Any client would want this vitality bestowed on his beloved products. Any client would entrust this woman with millions.

MATCHING PHILOSOPHIES

Bob made a short speech. Theoretically, it was for Amanda, but I felt it was really for Bob. He was already practicing how he would present her to new clients. And also how he would dazzle the old ones.

"Amanda, what I'm"—he corrected himself, remembering the CEO's presence in the room—"what *we're* really seeking is not just someone to step into the executive creative director position and keep everything on keel, but rather someone who can take the position, and in essence the very agency, into new directions. It's a highly visible office."

"Perhaps the most visible office in the system," Cliff graciously interjected.

Bob smiled and picked it back up. "The job comes with incredible opportunities to set the very pace and style by which this company will be judged. To fully demonstrate our new credo of Attract, Motivate, and Satisfy."

I glanced at Amanda and saw her pupils widen. These were her very words, and she recognized them. Philosophically, there was no doubt that she was a match for Bailey/Brumman/Lancaster.

■   ■   ■

THE MOMENT IS NOW

Bob continued. "It's an opportunity to be showcased and emerge at a seminal moment in our changing position in the advertising community. You know we're a privately held company. We have the money, the desire, *and* the foresight to change. What we need is"—he hesitated, and I thought he was going to say 'you, Amanda,' but he went on—"serendipity. The moment is now, Amanda."

I, of course, saw it as more than serendipity. I saw it as weeks of hard work, and years of preparation on all our parts for a moment like this. But if Bob—always the romantic—wanted to give it a name, I guess serendipity wasn't too bad.

Amanda stood. She knew the moment couldn't be topped and the meeting was over. She shook hands warmly with Bob and Cliff and me and was gone.

MEETING TED

The next day, Friday, the other three candidates were presented: two great guys and one "pompous asshole." They were all outstanding, but none of them came close to leaving the effect on Bob and Cliff that Amanda had. Bob liked them all, even the "pompous one," against his will. But his heart as well as his head had already been won by Amanda Kitchen. I suggested he meet Ted, Amanda's husband, before an offer was extended. Bob agreed with my advice that involving the whole family often smoothed a relocation.

Bob was ready to make an offer to Amanda. Bob was *more* than ready.

When I told Amanda that Bob wanted to meet Ted, she instantly invited him, my husband, and me to her home in Manhattan for dinner. The evening was a smash. Their housekeeper was from Mexico, and Bob and my husband, both products of the California school system, got to practice their high school Spanish with her. Amanda was radiant. Ted was a delight. Bob was, as always, open, direct, warm, and unafraid of risks, and now, all at once presidential. He sat to Amanda's right and it was not difficult to imagine the effect these two would have in tandem.

At one point during the evening, Bob and Amanda were talking about clients, my husband and the housekeeper were conjugating irregular verbs or something, and Ted and I found ourselves alone in the kitchen, getting coffee.

THE TWO-CAREER COUPLE

I asked him how he was feeling about all this.

"Well, it's wonderful of course," he said without hesitation. "I've never understood why people think that having two careers in one household poses a problem. She grows, I grow. I learn, stretch myself, I have more to offer her. And vice versa."

"Sounds very enlightened," I commented with a smile. Ted seemed to be that rare find—a supportive husband who recognized the value to each of them of their separate ambitions.

"But not so new," Ted continued. "I mean, Antony and Cleopatra both had careers!"

I laughed. "And Simone de Beauvoir and Jean-Paul Sartre both brought ideas home to each other."

Ted and I talked a bit more, and agreed to meet, just the two of us, the following week to discuss his options should things progress further.

On the way back to our hotel my husband remarked that every so often the world, or at least a small part of it, takes on a storybook quality. Surely it had appeared to happen that night.

The next morning Bob called.

"I've hardly slept because I'm so excited about Amanda! And my concerns regarding any 'husband' problems were completely put to rest after last night."

PULLING OUT ALL THE STOPS

Bob had already called Amanda to tell her more about the office in Los Angeles and the plans the company had for upgrading the premises while they upgraded the product: their advertising. He finished with, "Let's bring her to Los Angeles, BarBara. I'll meet her there and introduce her to our people."

Naturally, I was pleased but not too surprised by Amanda's call as I arrived for work Monday morning.

Amanda was eager to tell me all about her conversation with Bob Johnson. They had spoken about all his personal goals, how they could build the office together, the very dramatic change the company was embarking upon. And most important, he had ruled out the other candidates and was interested only in Amanda. He would hire Ted in a flash if that's what they wanted. If they thought it would be easier working in separate agencies, then Bob or I would find him a suitable position. Bob was pulling out all the stops.

"BarBara, I really want this position," Amanda finished. "It's just the kind of challenge and authority I want."

THE ONLY ONE IN THE RACE

I believed that informing Amanda that she was the sole candidate was a foolish thing for Bob to do. While I appreciated his enthusiasm, I always encourage our clients to keep their options open at this stage. It is also not a correct message to give the candidate. It is best that the individual not believe he or she is the only one capable or available or desirable to do the job. It clouds the issue and puts the employer at a disadvantage.

I would tell Bob this later, but at the moment the deed had been done. Actually, it didn't seem to matter. Amanda and Ted were both thrilled at the prospect of the move, the opportunities, the challenges. The whole situation still had that undeniable storybook quality—a bit of a glow. Everything seemed to be proceeding very smoothly.

TED'S OPTIONS

I was eager to meet with Ted individually for two reasons: It had been my experience that husbands and wives frequently presented different stories when they were away from their spouses, and I also wanted to assure Ted that we would treat his career with appropriate focus, not just as an add-on.

Conveniently, Ted and I were both in Chicago the next Tuesday, and he suggested lunch in our offices.

I liked Ted. It would be impossible not to. He was direct, straightforward, and he met your eyes as he shook your hand. He was solid and comfortable and definitely good-looking. He laughed often and without self-consciousness. I appreciated that he had suggested having lunch in, rather than at a restaurant, and he had arrived right on schedule. I could feel the slight tension draining from my shoulders. Ted was not going to sing a different tune. The whole situation was right on target, running smoothly.

The question was, what were Ted's legitimate options? I reviewed his résumé and the contents of his folder (which included comments we had accumulated about him from others at Jones & Livingston). He was an excellent candidate in his own right and shouldn't be thought of as just a part of Amanda's package. Not for a minute.

Over lunch Ted and I talked about his background, his successes, his situation at J&L, why he liked his work so much. "So you see, BarBara, what I really need now is to get into some mainstream advertising. I have to have that experience in order to move on."

"Yes, I know, Ted. It's still the necessary ingredient. Without it you don't have the credentials to make it much closer to the top."

CATCH-22

"I know that's why I'm stuck at J&L. My last promotion was designed only to assuage my restlessness. I got a different title and more money but nothing was really any different. It's a catch-22 situation: They can't move me without the proper background and I'll never get the proper background if they don't allow me to move."

"Ted, I know I can get you on the right accounts in Los Angeles. You have what they need—service account expertise—and they're very big in that on the Coast, everything from avocados to raisins has its own board and advertising needs. You will also have some sensational advertising from J&L that L.A. hasn't seen. Your work will look fresh and new and exciting to them. We can make it happen in a way that you use your experience as the wedge to get what you really want. In L.A. there will be a mutual need between you and an agency. In New York, by contrast, the needs are all yours and the options are few." Although the catalyst for this move was the opportunity presented to Amanda, there was no question that a move to Los Angeles could dramatically advance Ted's career, too.

■ ■ ■

MARRIED PARTNERS

I reflected on how difficult it often seemed to engineer what the women's magazines term "having it all." Even when both members of a couple support independent career growth, the realities of the marketplace frequently make their mutual goals difficult to achieve, especially when relocation is involved. This, however, was a textbook case of a truly win-win situation. *Savvy* magazine would have a field day with Amanda Kitchen and Ted Spencer.

". . . And that's what makes me tingle," Ted was saying. "The thought that Amanda and I are going to build our careers together in Los Angeles. *Los Angeles.*" His face lit up like a child's.

I smiled and said softly, "You're really happy about all this, aren't you, Ted?"

"And then some! Los Angeles is like a dream city to me. It's the cutting edge of everything that's happening. Every new idea seems to emanate from there."

He looked up with that handsome, open face. "I never get tired of living the dream. Amanda is that dream, too."

"Tell me about that," I prompted.

"I always wanted to marry a partner, a true peer, not a dependent woman. My mother was a dependent woman. She never even knew what my dad earned. She didn't know how to make out a check. I wasn't interested in a woman who didn't have her own life—I knew first hand how diminishing that can be. My friends and I had similar concerns, however, about marrying career women in our fields. What happens if she gets promoted over you? Or commands a higher salary? Is the marriage threatened? Then I met Amanda, and she was already more successful than I was." He laughed out loud. His easy, assured laugh was contagious. "She was even at the same agency. There was no chance for secrets. And best of all, it didn't matter. She's wonderful." He paused.

"Please go on, Ted. I don't hear enough of these conversations."

"Well, I was convinced that Amanda's position and her career success would put to rest all those concerns that my friends usually had. I would not suddenly call forth nasty old buried emotions I didn't know existed."

"And you were right?"

"Absolutely. Amanda and I are truly partners. We share. We reflect on each other. We motivate each other to be our best. We revel in each other's successes. And you know what? It's really helped us both to be in the same field but with different perspectives."

A CONTEMPORARY COUPLE

Susan came to the conference room door as if she had sensed that the conversation would never get better, and it was the moment to interrupt. "You have a two o'clock, BarBara." I went to my two o'clock meeting thinking about Ted. Why couldn't the world be full of guys like that? (Of course, there'd be no daytime soaps, and popular fiction would be reduced to stories about boys and their dogs.)

Things were finally beginning to change in the business world—not to mention what was starting to happen with marriages—and I felt as if I were helping to point a contemporary couple in the right direction. For days afterward I kept humming "California, Here I Come."

ROOM AT THE TOP

There was something else about this opportunity for Amanda that filled me with hope for the future.

Cliff Eagleton had effectively created something that very rarely exists—room at the top. He had reorganized the company and established an international planning committee that would ultimately include twenty members—only twelve of whom were firmly in place.

This meant that B/B/L had a calling card that would enable them to compete with any other agency for top talent. They could offer positions of real power. Someone newly hired for an upper-level position could strive for a policy-making seat on that twenty-person committee. Once there, that person would have impact with international scope.

With the position being offered her, Amanda would be at an agency that provided her with dramatic growth potential. At J&L she was blocked from upper management. At B/B/L she had a definite shot at occupying a power seat in the world of advertising.

THE GOOD LIFE

My office made arrangements for Amanda and Ted to fly to the Coast that next weekend. Bob Johnson and his wife would meet them there. It was hard to tell who was more excited: Certainly Ted and Amanda had cause to be, but Bob and his wife, Sylvia, were returning to what they had always considered home.

Ted called me first thing Monday morning to report on the weekend's events and extol the virtues of Los Angeles. (I told him he could have gotten a job as civic booster, but he was determined to pursue the original plan.) He was eager to return to L.A. for any interview I could help him set up, and even made it clear that he would be more than happy to pop for his own transportation and expenses.

Bob Johnson called from New York, where he was still cleaning up his old duties and preparing for the switch to the

Coast. He would be moving out there within a week; Sylvia and the kids—and the dog, who, miraculously, was no longer feeling morose—would follow when they sold their big house in Connecticut. He would be at the Los Angeles office starting the following week and wanted Amanda there as soon as possible.

"If Amanda wants to come out to meet other people here, and look at more houses, I told her to just do it. I'll be waiting for her."

AN EMOTIONAL SIGNAL

It's a common courtesy and certainly a protocol of our business that the participating parties keep one another up to date on events of significance. Ted had done this. Bob had, too.

Amanda didn't call.

I gave her a couple of days. There were a lot of reasons: She could have been tired from the trip, the baby could be sick, she may have had much to catch up on at J&L. And yet, how far away from a phone can you get?

I finally called her at home after my messages to her office remained unanswered. I asked her why I had not heard from her.

She said she wanted to get together with me *after* Ted completed his scheduled interviews. She then related many of the things about the trip that I had already covered with Ted and Bob. Amanda provided no new news and, unnervingly, no personal opinion. She said she was very busy at the office but would call to set up something definite.

Amanda had stated she wanted this position, but I couldn't help detecting a slight avoidance, which often is a signal of an emotional change of direction.

■ ■ ■

SECOND THOUGHTS?

I called Bob Johnson just before he left New York to express
my concern. Bob said he would schedule a meeting for the
three of us and present the offer to Amanda personally. Originally, he had asked me to present it to her alone, but because
I sensed an avoidance on her part, we both felt it would be
better if he met with her as well.

I didn't know if Amanda's apparent resistance was indicative of a subtle negotiating ploy or if she was actually having
second thoughts. And, if so, why? We made a date for dinner.
Ted was working late and would try to join the three of us for
dessert.

AMANDA'S CHANCE

The formal offer was astounding in its scope. Nothing was
overlooked. Amanda would walk in the door with the title of
senior vice-president/executive creative director. Her base
salary would be $250,000, with a guaranteed bonus of
$50,000 and stock options in two years. B/B/L would pay all
relocation expenses. Perks included a car and membership in
two exclusive clubs—a business club and a health club.

Best of all, Amanda would have full hiring and firing responsibilities and the authority to build her department as she
saw fit. This was the independent power Amanda said she
wanted. The agency was organized so that all production staff
also reported to her, allowing her greater control of the final
product. What an opportunity! Even more legend-building
than turning around a failing brand is turning a ho-hum
agency into a creative nova. This would be Amanda's charge.
Amanda's chance.

And one more thing. Assuming certain performance checkpoints—which were realistically within Amanda's abilities to reach and surpass—in two years Amanda would be offered a seat on the international planning committee.

"Will you put all of this in writing? In a letter of intent?" Amanda asked with the subtle assurance of knowing the answer.

"Hell, I'll have it typeset and bound in leather," Bob insisted in his charming but persistent way.

I was growing a little concerned that Amanda might have been offered too much. "I'm sure a simple and direct letter of intent will suffice, Bob. Don't you agree, Amanda?"

She did.

Bob ordered champagne, and we settled back for the fun parts; the specifics of timing, and press releases. Even a press conference would be warranted, because Amanda's hire signaled a turning point in two ways: She was part of a new era indicative of creative excellence and creative leadership. Second, she would very possibly be the first woman with real power in the arena of international advertising. Certainly a party would be held at the local ad club to welcome Amanda to the city. It was heady.

Amanda brought up only one stumbling block and Bob not only solved it on the spot but managed to capitalize on it. Amanda said she was not quite ready to return to work full-time. She wanted more time to be with the baby and felt these were particularly precious days.

"Amanda," I said, "hadn't you planned to be back at work full-time by now at J&L?"

"Yes, but I've changed my mind. I want another six months of half days."

I was concerned by this change of direction. Might this be an avoidance tactic? But before I could question her further, Bob jumped right in with a solution. Bob said he would put her on *full* salary immediately *and* give her six months at half days, providing she would agree to be in on any new business pitches that took place during that time.

She agreed on the spot.

Bob assured her the half-days arrangement would not pose a problem in running the creative department, as there was a creative services director who had been with B/B/L for many years. He could continue to handle the administrative aspects of the creative department. He'd "keep things running" and showcase Amanda at the same time.

I was very impressed by Bob Johnson's openness to Amanda's half-days request. It was just this type of flexibility and support that Amanda had told me was lacking at J&L/ New York since Tony Fortuna had been promoted to the Dallas office. I was even more impressed that Bob believed in Amanda's ability to run the department and get the job done, that he believed it was a long-term partnership, and was prepared to back all that up with full salary.

In contrast, J&L had slashed Amanda's $150,000 salary to $75,000 with only a $10,000 bonus in response to her being on half days. B/B/L was a classy company. They would be paying Amanda $300,000 (salary and bonus) for her mind and her commitment, *not* for her hours in the office. With her acceptance, her effective earning capacity would jump $215,000 while her time at home with the baby stayed the same. It was beautiful.

Ted called the restaurant to say that he wasn't going to finish in time to join us. Amanda announced that she wanted to share with Ted the excitement of the evening. She would call in the morning with her answer—the first indication to Bob and me that everything preceding was not as final as we had considered it to be. I confronted her on this delay.

"Amanda, *this* is the moment to make certain the offer is mutually agreeable. Is there any consideration—personally or professionally—that is still up in the air for you?"

She responded with a warm smile. "BarBara, Bob, everything's terrific. You go ahead and draw up that letter of intent. As I said, I'll call in the morning." She smiled broadly, shook both our hands, and left.

Bob and I finished the rest of the champagne. We should have been happier.

STUMBLING BLOCKS

Again, Amanda didn't call. Amanda could not be reached at work and no one answered at home. I called Ted at his office. When he heard it was me, the words came out in a tumble. He said that Amanda felt she would be too far from home in Los Angeles to drop in and see the baby and they would have to find a new housekeeper.

There was *some* truth to that. In New York they lived in a fabulous apartment they had bought when they married. It was fine with a new baby, and there was plenty of room for Corazon, their housekeeper. Amanda and Ted *walked* to work. If something went wrong with the baby, they were less than five minutes away. In Los Angeles they had their hearts set on something big and Spanish and rambling, preferably in Westwood. Suddenly a commute would separate them from their baby.

I reached Bob on the Coast. He was behaving more presidential by the minute, and said these were only details.

"BarBara, these are only *details*. There's nothing here that can't be overcome. Hell, I'll provide her with a nursery right next to her office." And then, as an afterthought: "It'll be right next to mine, too. I like that. We can relocate Corazon right along with the rest of the family. If necessary, I'll pick up Corazon's salary, too. Amanda can stay home with the baby in the mornings and bring both the baby and the housekeeper with her in the afternoons. Wherever Ted ends up can't be too far from our offices, unless he's in the Civic Center. They can all go home together at the end of the day. I can already picture coverage of this in the Home section of the Sunday *Times.* I'll make that baby famous." He laughed. "Corazon will probably go on to write cookbooks. Now, BarBara, will you knock some sense into those sweet kids for me? I've really made an offer no woman could refuse."

"There's no doubt about that, Bob, it's an incredible offer. But I'm afraid 'sense' is not the issue here. Amanda has been putting up a lot of obstacles and I want to make sure they are not excuses for something we don't understand. It is important for me to address what Amanda herself stated she wanted, and to make sure she meant what she said."

He was right, the offer was without precedent—at least in my experience nothing had even come close to this total commitment from an employer to meet whatever needs arose. And most of all, it more than supported Amanda's goal toward power. It gave her the freedom to exercise her power with all the everyday problems removed.

. . . IF ALL ELSE FAILS

"Tell Amanda she's doing it for the rest of the women out there," Bob continued. "Goddamnit, BarBara, appeal to her patriotism if all else fails." We both broke into laughter in spite of the seriousness of the situation.

It began to look like an appeal to patriotism might be in order: Amanda still hedged. I reminded Amanda of our earliest conversation. She had said, "I want to have an influence on this business. This is important work I do, and I want to be important, too, to have the largest reach possible. I want the power to affect change." I asked if she had changed her goals. She assured me that she hadn't. But first she wanted to check the agency out with friends and past employees. I encouraged her to do so but reminded her also that the very thrust of the agency was changing with its new management team—a team of which she would be an integral part.

Bob talked to Cliff Eagleton about Amanda's inexplicable

reluctances and confided his concerns and determinations. Cliff called me and asked if I could set up a meeting with him, Amanda, and me.

Cliff was brilliant. He sincerely spoke of his personal vision for the company and how he would infuse it into the agency of the next century. He cast Amanda as a large part of the dream and the reality. I have rarely been more impressed with a man speaking from his heart but using every quality of his intellect.

CHOOSING ADVISORS

Amanda sat motionless for what seemed like an eternity and then stood and announced, "I'm sorry, but I can't accept the position." She was ready to leave when I blurted out, "Wait a minute, Amanda. You owe all of us an explanation."

She said she had heard some "bad things about the agency," but wouldn't be specific. I asked her to whom she had talked in making her decision. Her answers were revealing. She had talked at length, she told us, to the human resource director at J&L. That was both unwise and unreliable. *He* obviously would not want to lose her. It wouldn't make him look good. And after all, both agencies would be pitching the same business from their Los Angeles offices. Clearly, he would not want Amanda suddenly to be working for the other side.

She also had talked with someone recently fired by Bob Johnson. It seemed that Amanda had gone to great lengths to find excuses and rationalizations.

She also volunteered that she had talked to her *mother.* Her mother's concerns were only for the baby. She had never wanted Amanda to work at all "while the children were young," whether at J&L or B/B/L.

If Amanda had set out to destroy this opportunity, she couldn't have turned to a better group of advisors.

PICKING UP THE PIECES

"Amanda," I asked, "do you think there is a reason you sought the advice only of people you knew would try to discourage you from this move?"

"I chose to talk with people I trust."

I mentioned three or four others I thought Amanda would trust, including Ted, but the more we logically and rationally recapped the issues and the opportunity, the less sense she made of her refusal. And Amanda was not to be dissuaded. The CEO did not want to give up, and he couldn't believe that *she* did. I recognized the moment of no return before he did and finally had to say there was nothing more to discuss. I believed Amanda was making a grievous career mistake and it appeared she would come to see it too late.

Interestingly, Ted called me the very next morning.

"BarBara," he began, "I think Amanda's making a big mistake, and I don't understand it at all. Is there anything I can do to help this situation?"

"What has she said to you about it, Ted?"

"Basically, that it just doesn't feel right to her somehow. But she was so high on this when we were in L.A. househunting! This makes no sense to me. I've never known her to be like this."

"She's turned to some interesting people for advice," I prompted.

"You said it! She's talked to two people at J&L, for God's sake. That puts *me* in a helluva position at work, too. Now they might not take *me* as seriously, knowing I wanted to move. Amanda even told the personnel guy, 'Oh, Ted's all for it.' "

Ted was sounding quite exasperated. Unfortunately, I was as baffled as he, and had no concrete solution. I did suggest that ultimately they would both benefit if Amanda could voice the real reasons underlying her actions.

WORKING FULL-TIME

Amazingly, Amanda went back to work at J&L full-time a week after she turned down the offer. Her full-time salary had been reinstated, but she had been moved to a smaller office in keeping with her reduced status at J&L, and she had no team reporting to her. I've never gotten satisfaction from saying "I told you so." Consequently, Amanda's situation at J&L only saddened me and added to my confusion regarding the whole loss.

RATIONALIZATIONS

What could this have been about? I went over the issues again in my mind:

- It had nothing to do with the opportunity itself. The position was clearly a major advancement with an open top and double the money.
- It had not been life-style. Los Angeles was their chosen dream city.
- Childcare was not the issue. B/B/L was to build a nursery right next to her office, pay for Corazon, and give Amanda another six months of half days at full salary. (Clearly, that had never been a legitimate issue of hers, as she did not hesitate to go back full-time at J&L right away.)

- Ted certainly wasn't standing in the way. *His* career would have been enhanced, and he was all for Amanda taking this position.

I knew that all the reasons Amanda had given were rationalizations at best and smoke screens for sure. But what was she endeavoring to conceal? I didn't have a handle on the emotional forces that held her back. She couldn't be afraid of succeeding beyond Ted—she'd done that for years and their marriage had not only survived, but thrived. Her mother's only concern was "for the children," and the new job would have made that better. Some people are just not risk-takers, but Amanda had never demonstrated this fear. She had relocated earlier in her career, and was a known turnaround artist. I couldn't come up with one single reason for this sad loss. This opportunity was what Amanda had said she wanted—and more. *So* much more.

POWER FAILURE

This was indeed Power Failure as I had come to define it. A woman stated clearly that she wanted power. She had the talent and savvy and background to get a shot at it. She actively sought it. She was offered a position of power with future potential. And turned it down.

I had been encountering Power Failure for many years before this incident with Amanda Kitchen. It struck me that hers was a complex case. The underlying factors were not at all clear to me. In fact, I had no idea how to begin to explain it.

The mystification I felt about Amanda's decision only reinforced my determination to discover the truth. I hoped that in time I would learn more about her life, and what motivated her choices. This was not a woman who seemed stuck in the roles and rules of a previous generation.

But it would be another full year before I was to discover the truth—the subconscious barrier that short-circuited her rise to the top and caused her Power Failure.

However, my list of women who committed Power Failure was burgeoning, and my understanding of the phenomemon was growing.

Amanda's Power Failure was hardly an isolated incident—only a highly dramatic example that left many unanswered questions in its wake.

These are questions we should all be asking of ourselves, our culture, and each other. The answers will not come easily. There will be confusion and obfuscation and continual resistance, because change is never easy. And few truly seek it.

Amanda eventually did. But not before the bitter aftertaste of Power Failure forced the exposure of the truth.

In my experience, all women who overcome or avoid Power Failure have to face themselves and their choices through four distinct steps:

1. Recognition of the problem
2. Acceptance of responsibility for solving the problem
3. Discovery of the genesis—the root—of the problem
4. Transcendence: owning one's own power

Amanda eventually faced the issues underlying her Power Failure and the psychological truths so specific to her gender. Today, she is once again on her way to corporate power, and I will reveal later her struggle and her transcendence.

Not all women make it. There are hundreds, maybe even thousands, who have stood at the threshold of corporate power and could not, would not, take the final step.

In addition to Amanda Kitchen, I will relate the stories of

five of them: Maria Stollenwerk, Vicki Dennison, Mary Louise DeVaney, Catherine Ames, and Sandy Auerbach. Like Amanda, each one of them suffered Power Failure. Unlike Amanda, not all of them faced and conquered Power Failure.

The purpose of this book is to reveal this hidden epidemic: the phenomenon of Power Failure.

THE PHENOMENON OF
POWER FAILURE

■

VERY FEW women get to the top.

Very few women even have aspirations for the top.

Not many expect ever to run a division of a major corporation. Fewer still expect to fill the CEO's position. However, there are women who have stated emphatically that these were *their* aspirations, *their* goals. These women were determined to let nothing prevent them from reaching the top. And then, when this well-deserved prize was within their grasp, they gave it away. From these contradictions of stated purpose and ultimate actions emerges the opportunity for rare insights into why women are so underrepresented at the top and how we are all affected by their Power Failure.

WHERE ARE THE WOMEN WHO'VE MADE IT?

In April of 1984, the cover of *Fortune* magazine presented one of the most puzzling and compelling social issues of our time: "Why Women Aren't Getting to the Top." Two years later the August 1986 cover of *Fortune* featured the headline "Why Women Are Bailing Out." Virtually every major magazine and newspaper has explored this issue over the last few years. Their speculations, or at best, hypotheses, have all been different, and rarely satisfactory. The September 12, 1988 issue of *Fortune* continued to report on the overdue "upward mobility" of women into senior corporate ranks. *Fortune* interviewed many senior male executives at decidedly pro-female companies, one of whom stressed that his company's plan "has no magic solutions to lower the high dropout rate of corporate women; no one has."

Feminists, business professors, psychologists, and business leaders are all searching to discover the factors that lead men but very few women to reach the upper career rungs. Explanations range from blatant sexism to the lack of role models, from boardroom members who "don't feel comfortable with women" to inadequate day care facilities, from not being allowed in Little League to not being allowed in the executive washroom.

Everyone seems to be asking, "Where are the women who've made it?" The August 1986 *Fortune* article reports these grim statistics:

> A 1985 study of 401 women who received MBAs between 1973 and 1982 from the University of Pittsburgh found that 18% were either unemployed or working only part-time. Moreover, 34% of the women had dropped out of the labor force at one time or another, compared with 19% of the

men. Among graduates of New York's Pace University who received their MBAs between 1976 and 1980, 21% of the women are not working full-time, compared with only 1% of the men.

Fortune continues by noting the dearth of women in senior positions. They cite a Korn/Ferry International study:

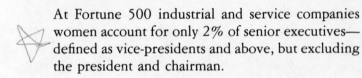 At Fortune 500 industrial and service companies women account for only 2% of senior executives— defined as vice-presidents and above, but excluding the president and chairman.

Business Week, October 23, 1987, reports in its special issue *The Corporate Elite* that only two of the CEOs of the Business Week 1,000 are women.

When you consider that women comprise more than 50 percent of the population, this figure is shocking.

Ann Morrison, Randall White, and Ellen Van Velsor, authors of *Breaking the Glass Ceiling,* concur:

In the Fortune 500 companies, only 1.7% of the corporate officers are women, according to a 1986 study by Mary Ann Von Glinow, a professor in the school of business at the University of Southern California.

. . . Despite increasing numbers of women in business, women are definitely underrepresented in the most powerful management positions.

As president of my own executive search and consulting firm specializing in the fields of marketing and advertising—long considered two of the most promising fields for women— these statistics dismay but don't surprise me.

■　■　■

I NEVER QUESTIONED IT

When I was very young I was hired as the receptionist for a medium-size manufacturing company, because I was "blonde and pretty." However, I was also ambitious and curious, although these characteristics did not carry the same weight as their more visible counterparts.

Because everyone knows and talks to the receptionist—and I was an eager listener who had occasion to access the entire premises—I slowly absorbed many of the fundamentals of that particular company: the purchasing agent delighted in sharing the details of a significant coup that saved thousands of dollars; assembly-line workers took justified pride in demonstrating cost-effective shortcuts; truck drivers showed extraordinary patience when instructing an intimidated novice in the intricacies of parking an 18-wheeler; the skills employed by welders and spray-painters approached art.

When I asked if there was more I could do, the answer was, "Payables and receivables." Within a year I was the full-charge bookkeeper. A year after that I was appointed comptroller.

And then, five years into a productive career with that company, when I joyfully announced to the owners that I was pregnant, they fired me. In the same conversation it was clear that they assumed I would be responsible for finding, interviewing, and training my replacement. The man hired, incidentally, never set foot in the factory or understood the work or the workers, but nevertheless started at a much higher salary than I had been earning.

This was a difficult time.

My husband was a full-time college student with a most demanding course load and he was nearing graduation. He had dropped out of school for two semesters to earn the extra money we would need for the baby. My insurance at work did not include coverage of any of the costs of pregnancy or childbirth. We needed my income.

I could have continued in my position with just the slightest interruption, but my employers didn't see it that way. The way they saw it, women could work until they became too obviously pregnant, then, bingo, their time was up. It didn't matter to them how good I was at my job, or how committed I was to the company, or how much I needed to work—I was pregnant. They never believed I would return after I "had a baby." When I reminded them, "My husband's a student, I plan to keep working," their response was, "You say that now, Bar-Bara, but you'll feel differently when you have a little baby at home." They firmly believed they knew better and were doing me a favor.

When I offered to stay until I could "close out the year," they readily accepted. I worked until 11:00 P.M. on my last day, New Year's Eve.

In retrospect, what bothers me the most about being fired is that I went along with it. I never thought to fight it. I found and trained my replacement. I never questioned it. That was just the way it *was.*

Ten days into January I gave birth to our daughter. Two weeks later I started a new job.

Eventually I had to ask myself why I had acquiesced to an event I found philosophically unacceptable although it was culturally imperative. If there had been a profoundly evident failure, then who would claim it for himself? Or herself? Who would give it a name? What would this lack of personal empowerment be called?

Eventually, I came to accept personal responsibility for my passive role at that juncture. I came to feel peace about its ramifications, and renewed vigor about my power to create my own life, regardless of cultural barriers or expectations of my gender.

That was the early sixties, and the world has changed dramatically since then. We are so aware of the altered cultural biases, the increased opportunity, the new successful woman. And yet women are still not reaching the top. Why don't the statistics match our current perceptions?

THE RISING STARS

This book tells the stories of six women who came very near the top. And could have gone further.

All appeared—to the business world at large, to the trade press, to women lower on the ladder—to have "made it." All were earning six-figure salaries. All held important managerial positions.

Yet all had short-circuited their careers before taking the prize literally held out to them: a place at the very top. It is my hope that the truth behind these women's stories will be illustrative for us all.

Our clients retain us to identify and attract qualified candidates appropriate for key executive positions. Bools & Associates then functions as the negotiator between client and executive, to develop a mutually beneficial outcome.

Last year I placed executives in presidencies, international planning positions, and number-two and -three positions of numerous companies worldwide. Notably, although I regularly presented highly qualified female candidates, *not one of the people who finally moved into these top spots was a woman.*

I know what constitutes a fast track and what constitutes a dead end. I know what top management looks for in hiring. I know what a key executive needs in his or her next career move.

In 1976 I began a private survey. I identified ten women in marketing and advertising who were up-and-coming "stars."

Powerful, confident, extremely good at both the tangibles and the intangibles of their work, they seemed destined for the corridors of power. They were rising marketing whizzes in major companies, or exciting creative talents in advertising agencies with an ability to sell their work and nurture their juniors, or account executives with a powerful overview of marketing and a broad view of how to increase their clients' business.

Five years later not one of them had made it to the top. In fact, only one of them was even still in the business.

I was shocked at this realization. Then I reasoned that the seventies were still a difficult time for women. Things would be different in the eighties.

My clients were actively seeking talented, capable women in the upper levels, and so again I needed to target the rising stars. It wasn't hard. The few women with big responsibilities and big titles, earning big salaries, are extremely visible. They get lots of media attention. Their progress is watched by the whole business.

SEARCHING FOR PATTERNS

Some years after my first awareness of executive women falling off the fast track, Lydia Swan joined me in identifying the characteristics and actions of the rising female stars of the eighties. I had accumulated extensive notes on dozens of cases—Lydia had a background in psychology and a gift for writing. Lydia's own experience as a recruiter at Bools & Associates had quickly convinced her of the pervasiveness of women nearing, but not reaching, the top. We were most interested in the women who *could* have made it: women who stated they wanted power, actively sought it, were offered it, and turned it down. In choosing representative stories, we eliminated the hundreds of women who were ambivalent about their careers, or who expressed no tangible goals of reaching top policy-making positions. This still left us with dozens of women who were passionate about their work and their goals, who nevertheless forfeited the opportunity for power when it was offered to them.

Lydia and I began to search for patterns. My notes about each of these executive women were very detailed—exact conversations, childhood memories, attitudes about spouses or partners, her children, her company, her bosses, her dreams and ambitions. I also had full career histories, references from superiors and peers and a clear understanding of the milieu in which these women lived and worked. In many cases I had met their husbands or partners, bosses and co-workers in the course of my involvement with them.

Julia Targ, our consulting psychologist on the project, told us that social scientists often have difficulty gaining access to the type of women with whom we are in regular contact. Although at the time Lydia and I didn't fully appreciate what it would come to mean, we possessed rich information on scores of executive women.

Lydia and I studied gender psychology, modern anthropology, popular social commentary and dipped into the wealth of current business books. We began to identify the many differences in the way men and women think, love, and work that matched our own experiences and the experiences of the hundreds of women we had chronicled. The patterns we uncovered are the core of this book. We each had a passion to discover the truth about women who say "no" to top management positions.

In this book I present the stories of six such executive women. This is not an interview format or a survey or a presentation of women who sought therapeutic help. These six women were at the peak of their careers, and I was there.

In the course of my work I shared a time in their lives that was ripe with choices and chances. I got to know their careers intimately. I was able to assess their opportunities from a unique vantage point—that of knowing their marketplace better than they did. And to each of these women I presented insights and opportunities for advancement that would have furthered their careers, that would have brought them closer to the elusive and influential *top* spots they had insisted they wanted.

A HIDDEN PHENOMENON

Firsthand insights into the handful of women who have been considered for influential top positions afford us a rare and telling view of the interior motivations of some of business's best and brightest.

Let me stress the elusive nature of power positions—the positions these women were offered. Power is rarely offered but widely sought. Very few—men *or* women—ever reach the top of major corporations.

In this book I will reveal a hidden phenomenon very few have seen and almost no one believes exists: The opportunities are there, the offers are there, the women are not. In spite of the prevailing myths to the contrary, women are encouraged, sought after, absolutely *courted* for top leadership and policy-making posts. *And they are turning them down!*

Amazingly, all of the women in these stories stated—clearly and repeatedly—that they wanted power to impact their world, that they wanted to reach the top. Although they all achieved some measure of success, they all short-circuited their careers and gave away power.

■ ■ ■

POWER FAILURE

Big business is reaching out to the most talented women to place them in the top positions of power. Power these women *think* and *say* they want. However, these women literally say "no" to this power once it is offered. I call this very real phenomenon *Power Failure.*

To understand Power Failure, we must first clearly understand the nature of power—in the world and in ourselves.

THE NATURE OF POWER

Power is a force. It is the ability to do or act. It is the ability to mobilize resources—money, people—to influence results. It is the capacity to affect part of the world in which we live.

As such, power is neither good nor evil. It is neutral in value. Both Jesus and Hitler had power, and used it to affect different types of change, to rally people toward different ends.

Corporate and organizational power is similar in nature. In a corporate hierarchy, the ability to get things done translates to having the responsibility and authority to command people and spend money. Corporate power is measured in tangible, sometimes palpable terms: How many people does a given executive manage? How indispensable are those people? What are their combined salaries? How much revenue is that executive responsible for? How much profit? How much money does that position control?

Aspects of corporate power that are less easily measured include to what degree a given individual can affect changes not directly in his or her area of authority. How well does one garner the assistance of peers, the support of superiors? Into what profitable new areas does this individual lead the organization?

An important truth about power: It emanates from the individual. Certain posts carry a degree of corporate and political power, but it is the person who inhabits such a position who exercises it and makes his or her personal influence felt.

POWER AND SUCCESS

Power must be distinguished from success. As I've stated, power is a force, a vehicle. Success is a destination.

The dictionary defines success as "the favorable or prosperous termination of attempts or endeavors," and "the satisfactory accomplishment of something attempted." The definition of power is "the ability to do; capacity to act; capability of performing or producing."

Power is a process, a way of choosing. Success is closure, attainment, already having.

In corporate life, success is a symptom. Money, title, perks—these are symbols of success, and while they may indicate who has power and who does not, they are not, and should not be mistaken for, power itself.

Having thus differentiated power from success, the question arises, "Why want power?" The personal benefits of success are clear—money, comfort, prestige. What are the benefits of power?

Herb Cohen, world-renowned negotiator, in his best-selling book *You Can Negotiate Anything,* talks of personal power this way:

> [Power] is indispensable for mental health and nonaggressive survival. . . . You have plenty of

power. Use it to sensibly implement objectives that are important to you. You owe it to yourself not to live by what someone else thinks you ought to do.

Business consultant Antony Jay, in *Management and Machiavelli* writes:

The real pleasure of power is the pleasure of freedom, and it [is] one of man's most primitive needs, the need to control his environment.

POWER AND VISION

Exercising power is synonymous with effectively expressing one's own ideas and visions. Imagine two executives with conflicting views in a given corporation: One desires to structure a cooperative, accessible management team; the other believes productivity is enhanced by fostering competitive factions within the organization. Power will determine the outcome. Another corporate leader might believe that a portion of the work force could effectively do their jobs at home, thereby eliminating the costs of commuting, wardrobe, and childcare. Power enables him or her to implement this. Or consider the corporate executive who believes that American bureaucracies are cumbersome compared to foreign corporations, and has ideas on how to restructure. Power is needed to get it done.

When an individual leader develops and then champions a certain vision, there is tremendous power in action. It is the stuff of long-term corporate heroes, according to Terrence Deal and Allan Kennedy in *Corporate Cultures:*

Perhaps most importantly, heroes provide a *lasting influence within the organization.* The values of

Thomas Watson, Charles Steinmetz, General Johnson, and William Cooper Procter still provide the glue that bonds the great organizations they built. A favorite story of Ochs's at *The New York Times*— still told today—illustrates the point. The story concerns a traveler who in medieval times meets three stonecutters along a road and asks each of them what he's doing. The first says, "I am cutting stone." The second says, "I am shaping a cornerstone." But the third answers, "I am building a cathedral." The strength of *The New York Times* lies in the fact that its staff are cathedral builders, as Ochs encouraged them to be, not stonecutters.

Power is a vehicle to express one's unique vision in the world. When women are not at the top, the values they could be bringing to the workplace are lost.

POWER AT THE TOP

Being at the top requires power, and having sufficient power allows someone to be at the top. These concepts are intertwined.

In order to determine how *women* could obtain power, let's see how power is obtained.

To begin with, power is assumptive. A powerful person believes he or she *has* it, is *entitled* to it, and knows his or her ideas and goals are as valid, if not better, than that of others.

The special issue of *Business Week* dated October 23, 1987 (featuring The Corporate Elite) quotes Abraham Zaleznik, a psychoanalyst and the Konsuke Matsushita Professor of Leadership at Harvard University. He suggests the mark of top executives is that they "constantly emit signals" that they have the right to be there.

Children of both sexes have traditionally been told that any little boy could become president. Most men don't doubt their own entitlement; most women do.

Next are goals of influence. What outcomes are desired, both short-term and long-term? How can one gain the power and authority to make these things happen? Power potential is within the individual, but the outcome is external.

Let's imagine a fast-rising executive on her way to the top. She has the desire to move part of her company's business into a new area. It's a calculated risk—that segment of the market is growing and profitable, but there is some competition ahead. Nonetheless, she has a vision. She knows this is the thing to do. To accomplish anything significant toward her goal, she will need massive support—people, dollars, the commitment of management. How does she get it? How does one obtain power?

Like anything else in life, one must endeavor to determine the realities of the game that is being played. Who has power? How do other people get it? First, an awareness of the game is critical, followed by a commitment to determine the realities of the workplace.

Many women enter the work force expecting it to be something other than what it is, hoping it will offer satisfaction and rewards. They would be better served by viewing the work world as an arena to develop—not "be provided"—their *own* satisfaction and rewards. Rather than illusory hope, women need to enter the work force with clear, basic questions:

- Why am I here?
- What is the game?
- How do I play the game?
- Where are the power centers of the corporation?

- How can I expand my responsibility and authority?
- How can I make the company more profitable?
- What are the goals of my organization?
- How do I relate my work to the health of my corporation, my industry?
- How far do I want to go?
- What criteria are involved in reaching top positions?

Above all, women need to ask, "What is the reality of the world I have chosen to enter?"

Psychiatrist M. Scott Peck, in his moving best seller *The Road Less Traveled,* talks about the importance of a dedication to reality:

> The more clearly we see the reality of the world, the better equipped we are to deal with the world. The less clearly we see the reality of the world—the more our minds are befuddled by falsehood, misperceptions and illusions—the less able we will be to determine correct courses of action and make wise decisions.

In my view, women don't dedicate themselves to uncovering the *truth* about the world of work. They work hard; they strive for success; they suffer when reality doesn't match expectation. But consistently, women's internal lives cause them to forgo top-level power, even when it is offered.

To begin to understand this phenomenon, we must look closely at some of the psychological differences between men and women.

■   ■   ■

WHERE DOES POWER FAILURE START?

It starts young. So young that none among us can recall the first time we said to our emerging self, "I am a girl" or "I am a boy" and grappled with what that meant.

In some ways it starts at birth. The first words spoken about the newborn are either "It's a boy!" or "It's a girl!" But the drama truly begins in toddlerhood. It is the toddler who starts to develop identity.

Identity. The classic "Who am I?" emerges during these brief years. Psychologically speaking, the toddler has two important developmental tasks to achieve: (1) individuation and (2) gender identity.

Individuation requires the development of an internal voice that says, "I am separate from others. I am a singular entity." The infant is bonded to the primary care giver—almost always a woman, for traditionally it is women who "mother"—and does not know its own selfhood. But with the freedom of walking and talking comes the realization of separateness, the fear of aloneness, the emergence of individuation.

Also crucial in the formation of identity is the toddler's task of gender identification.

- Am I male or female, and what does that mean?
- What tasks, roles, rules, and expectations fit my gender?
- From whom will I learn these?
- After whom will I model my behavior, my desires?

Because it is primarily women who raise children in these early years, the differential development of gender identity in boys and girls travels significantly different paths.

Every time Mother says to a son, "No, you can't carry my purse; only girls carry purses," or "No, you can't be a mommy when you grow up; only girls have babies. You can be a daddy," the little boy is slapped with the awareness that he is separate (and fundamentally different) from his most significant "other" (from Mother), that he is not to be part of her club, cannot duplicate her experience in his own life. That he is fundamentally *other than.*

Whereas boys are thrust early into an awareness of their separateness (thus making individuation consciously imperative), for girls, the identification with the mother is more continual. Rather than the shock of separateness that boys experience, girls glide more slowly into awareness of selfhood. And while boys must look beyond that initially powerful primary care giver for information on male behavior (struggling to learn what it is to be a man from the relatively elusive parent who is male, from other little boys, from rejecting what within them seems feminine), girls look to their mothers for the meaning and experience of their own feminine nature, never having to leave the initial primary "other" to learn about the roles and rules of their gender.

Throughout childhood and beyond, the predominant structure and pattern of same-sex play differs between males and females. "Boys' " games require greater skill acquisition than do most "girls' " games, and they adhere far more to structure and regulation. These games are typically competitive; boys play games with rules. They play to win, whether their best friends are teammates or opponents. Arguments are settled by abiding by rules of play, tentative bonds between playmates maintained by adhering to principles and regulations that supersede the individual people involved.

Girls' play groups are usually smaller and more intimate than those of boys. Their games and peer relationships are generally based on assumptions of trust and mutuality rather than rules and individuality. When disputes develop among girls, the game itself is often dropped, as they are unwilling to risk losing the warm feelings of peership and cooperation. Girls show a greater willingness than boys to bend rules, make exceptions, and adapt to innovations. However, failing conciliation by these means, girls feel a lack of guidelines and often are unable to return to play. In this way, they can be left vulnerable to feelings of betrayal and loss. Girls endeavor to preserve relationships, which they intuitively feel to be more salient than any rules of play.

And here we arrive at the clearest single division between the ways in which men and women typically approach choices, problems, life.

Men are *situational.* Women are *relational.*

Independence versus intimacy. Separateness versus connectedness. This is one of life's overriding themes, one that each of us grapples with countless times each day.

While we all live with some sense of individual identity as well as some sense of collective identity, there are significant differences in the ways men and women mature in regard to these themes.

The focus of male social development seems to be clear-cut: ever-increasing autonomy throughout childhood, adolescence, and young adulthood. The self must be discovered, nurtured, and respected in order to develop a singular identity, in order to achieve. A man will have people in his life during these years—family, friends, a lover—to be sure, but their value is weighed against their ability to help him achieve his personal goals. Once a man has established his individual identity, and is comfortable with the rules of play in the life of his choice, he is free to risk intimacy, commitment, relationships.

The female path is very different. Without a clear road to increased autonomy, a woman's psychological development shows *self* and *others* solidly intertwined. She first defines her self-worth by the success of her relationships, often even describing herself in terms of those relationships—Bill's wife, Susan's best friend, Jimmy's mother. Oftentimes, only when she is comfortable that she has the ability—as an adult woman—to engender and sustain important relationships will a woman feel free to discover and encourage her unique ambitions, to express her independent self.

Traditionally, women in their twenties and thirties concern themselves with developing and nurturing relationships—husband, children, friends—while men in these decades concentrate on setting and reaching their self-sought ambitions.

For many, these roles and focal goals begin to shift and converge in their forties and beyond. Questioning the ultimate value of their life's work, men may pull in, eager to feed their hearts, seeking greater degrees of intimacy in love and friendship. Women at this time feel freer to reach outside the family circle, wanting to explore a larger world, ready to be more masterful, more self-directed, and invest less of their energies in promoting other people's destinies.

It is generally not until midlife that men and women begin to investigate the half of the spectrum long relegated to the other sex. By this point, men as a group are exercising real world power, while women have made their mark by perpetuating the culture's values in the next generation. Through the most productive and influential years of their adult lives, men are *situational.* Women are *relational.*

WOMEN AND POWER IN HISTORY

Of course, it would be impossible to thoroughly discuss the entire subject of women's power and powerlessness through time. This brief review is meant to suggest that the development of a relational orientation was women's attempt to gain power by association when direct power was denied or not possible. Could it be that until the cultural upheaval of recent times, psycho-social divisions along gender lines developed out of the concern for survival?

For the thousands of years preceding the conventions of

civilization, survival depended upon having enough to eat and not falling prey to other hungry inhabitants of the wild. During pregnancy and nursing, women were definitely more at risk. Women with the ability to develop and sustain close emotional ties earned themselves protectors, and enhanced their chances at survival in a harsh environment.

After the start of recorded history, the rare woman has been able to exercise an impressive degree of power—female monarchs, from Cleopatra to the queens of England, ruled kingdoms, and Joan of Arc led armies. But these are unusual examples. The monarchs had lineage and precedence on their side, and Joan of Arc had God. But the vast majority of women were limited to *Kinder, Kuche, Kirche* (children, kitchen, church; the traditional triangle of women's sphere of activity).

Power and survival are closely related. In the eighteenth century, writer and critic Samuel Johnson quipped: "Nature has given women so much power that the law has wisely given them none." In the nineteenth century, industrialization deepened the division of labor between men and women. Men held power of the means of production and the market economy, which only intensified women's dependence on them for economic survival.

From *The Light of the Home* by Harvey Green, which *The Washington Post's Book World* described as ". . . a very disturbing inventory of the means by which woman's place has been defined," we have this analysis of the industrial era's cult of motherhood:

> Science, religion, and the political structure of late-nineteenth-century America formed a powerful force for inequality between men and women. There are two basic responses to situations of persistent inequality: the dominated sector can actively or passively resist, generally at great risk to itself; or the dominated sector can build elaborate intellec-

tual rationales for its position, and claim some future reward of a generally nonmaterial nature . . . the vast majority of middle-class women accepted their position.

Political and social power properly belonged to women only as maternal responsibility.

Motherhood was simultaneously endowed with enormous responsibility and limited authority . . . By valuing precisely those qualities of sentiment and community which social and economic reality denied or ignored, the cult of motherhood became an institutionalized, but powerless, conscience for capitalism.

In a world where the law gave women little, if any, power, and biology required they be tied to others, a relational orientation ensured survival. Viewed against this backdrop, women's development of a finely tuned sense of bondedness within intimate relationships was a strong move on behalf of their own survival. Women became indispensable as kin keepers, as protectors and nurturers of intimacy and connectedness, in order to exert a kind of power against the possibility of being alone.

The price of these bonds could be enormously high. A woman could not move from her father's house unless she moved into her husband's. Even if she earned money in her own right she still could not own property or vote. Widowhood and/or abandonment were constant threats.

Nevertheless, the power inherent in relationalism served women during the course of history. Power by association was often the closest women could get to the real thing.

■ ■ ■

THE PRICE OF RELATIONALISM

Today women have options previously unavailable. Centuries-old customs and traditions are changing with a startling rapidity. Public schooling provides the same education to girls as to boys. University admissions display as equal openness to female students as male. In many industries, women are increasingly represented in entry-level management positions. In some industries, more than half the management training hires are women. Although many women choose not to pursue high-level positions, the opportunities are there for them. *Fortune* magazine, September 12, 1988, reports that "Merck, Corning, Gannett, Capital Cities/ABC, and nearly forty other companies have established programs designed to retain and promote women to executive jobs." In my experience, there are also many companies that actively seek women for their highest ranks, even if they have not adopted a formal program.

And the law gives women rights undreamed of in previous centuries. Women now vote, own property, run for public office, live alone. Independence is no longer a rare privilege, it is a legal right.

Nonetheless, women continue to pay the price of an orientation that requires strong emotional bonds. Although the reality of life in the late twentieth century hardly supports it, women still tend to feel the loss of close emotional bonds as a threat to survival itself.

In *Unfinished Business,* psychologist Maggie Scarf draws these conclusions about why women show dramatically higher rates of depressive illness:

> It is the female's inherently interpersonal, interdependent, affiliative nature—her affectionateness and orientation toward other people—that underlies her far greater vulnerability. . . . Women are so very

> powerfully invested in their . . . relationships—and derive such a sense of self from these vital emotional connections—that their very inner selves become intertwined with other selves, the selves to which they've become so powerfully attached.'
> . . . It is in woman's willingness to put or ante up so much of her "self" into relationships that she places herself at so much greater risk.

Clearly, relationalism is a risky orientation. When women so "powerfully" include other people in their definition of self, they do so at the expense of an unquestioned sense of independent power. Those without an autonomous sense of self are prone to suffer depressive illness. Although historically a dependent arrangement may have helped ensure survival, today it is largely outmoded. Today, women *endanger* themselves by perpetuating expectations of external salvation in the form of a relationship. The woman who waits to be saved by the "knight in shining armor" risks so much more than just a long wait.

In the larger social world, the cost of relationalism is also evident. Accustomed only to power by association, women's personal power is rare. Without personal power, corporate power is all but impossible.

POWER FAILURE TODAY

Today the reality of life and work in post-industrial nations bears little resemblance to life and work in any other period of human history. Beryl Lieff Benderly makes this point in *The Myth of Two Minds,* her 1987 book on gender differences:

> Who had the stronger shoulders, who might unpredictably become pregnant, clearly meant a great

deal when work and warfare ran on muscle power and conception lay as far beyond human control as the weather. But now, when every American fingertip commands horsepower by the thousands, when the neighborhood drugstore and clinic offer freedom from fertility, those two great physical differences weigh very lightly indeed in the social balance.

The minds, energies and abilities of both men and women can be equally valuable to corporate and public policy, and to raising the next generation. The work of our culture no longer needs to be divided by sex. Internally, however, the old realities continue to influence our self-definition, our perceived role, and our behavior. Technology has outstripped consciousness.

Today I regularly see that women are being *offered* opportunities to participate and change the world. It often seems to me that they don't see them for the unprecedented, policy-making opportunities they are.

Often it is women themselves who sabotage their personal power, by continuing to operate in smaller, more comfortable worlds, even though this may be dysfunctional, antiquated behavior.

Many of the values generally associated with femininity and relationalism—kindness, nurturance, concern with the well-being and development of others, community, warmth, fostering intimacy, etc.—are important *human* values. Thus we make a distinction between relational *values* and a relational *orientation,* the root of which is the fear of losing relationships.

Power is best obtained and maintained by employing relational values *when appropriate* and situational strategies *when appropriate.* And having the wisdom to know the difference.

With a dedication to the reality of the situation, a leader is able to choose appropriately when to act with empathy or connectedness, fairness or control.

To do this, one must first trust one's own voice and believe in one's own goals and the right to see them come to fruition. Power must be owned by the individual.

Most women, however, include other voices in with their own. All too often, *above* their own. In contrast, leadership requires believing in one's own visions and taking responsibility for subsequent decisions. Leaders—the good ones, anyway—seek others' opinions when contemplating policy or action, but they do not gratuitously give those other opinions credence above their own.

Power and leadership require having a point of view, beliefs, goals. Power is the ability to act on them without fear of severing relationships. Leadership is imparting vision and goals to others and fostering their commitment to help achieve those ends.

Those at the top have visions, and move toward them through the unstinting use of power and leadership.

The women in these stories got as far as they did because they had large *external* visions (when they approached the world situationally) and consequently were able to express their beliefs on a broad canvas. They failed because they had small internal visions (when they operated with a relational orientation). Their own lives were always considered relationally, in terms of other people. Thus, the "other people" in each woman's internal constructs ultimately undermined her and determined her ceiling. Her own limits.

Obtaining and maintaining power requires both a large external vision and a large internal vision. Corporate, organizational power cannot be achieved without personal power.

To illustrate this, I have chosen the experiences of these six particular women. This is not a random or arbitrarily chosen group. These women had power on their agendas. They wanted it. They expected it. They demanded it. And they said so.

Let me show you, through the lives of these remarkable women, how a relational orientation works against women instead of for them, how their need for these relationships blinds them to the realities of the game, a game designed by those in power, those who are situational: men. Had they owned their own power without the fear of losing relationships, they could have written new rules and reached whatever goals they set for themselves. Internal power becomes external power.

Ultimately, these six women, and thousands like them, committed Power Failure in the workplace because they suffered Power Failure in themselves.

TOWARD LIFEPLACE

What do we stand to gain, as a society, if women are able to transcend the Power Failure within and assume positions of public authority?

It is my vision that eventually, the lines of workplace and homeplace will be erased, and we will have a *Lifeplace,* a place where our outmoded and strict orientations of relationalism and situationalism will be integrated, and both men and women will be able to foster connectedness and community while honoring contracts and situational rules of play.

Men and women would benefit from true equality; the integration of love and work, work and home that would be Lifeplace. All of the important tasks and values of our culture could be gender-free, chosen by individual proclivity and ability. Each person could be free to bring his or her visions and beliefs to the largest appropriate arena. Lifeplace would be a place where women could own their relational values rather than be owned by them, and men could be motivated by situational realities rather than driven by them.

Consider the idea of "bicultural" leadership presented by Susan Davis, vice-president at the Harris Bank (*Chicago Sun-Times,* February 14, 1988):

I've concluded that each leader—male or female—must become comfortable acting out of both systems of values so that the situation itself can dictate which behavior is appropriate. Instead, we as leaders more often choose the "cultural" behavior which is more comfortable to us. It is not always the best behavior for the particular challenge.

Each male and female leader must stretch and grow to become comfortable with both cultures and with both values. Then each leader's actions will match the challenge with the most appropriate solution.

Stronger leaders will guide their diverse colleagues and our institutions can prosper. As few rise to the challenge of the global economy, we will find the solutions we need. Men and women together will fashion solutions not now envisioned. We can make partnerships that last at home and at work.

Davis continues with vivid imagery of her beliefs:

To become more powerful leaders, men need to become more comfortable with finding the alternatives to taking the hill; women need to become more comfortable with taking the hill when there is no alternative.

It is a compelling opportunity we have at this point in human history: to integrate our values and our genders; to create Lifeplace.

■   ■   ■

THE CHALLENGE WITHIN

The road toward Lifeplace—the choice to grow or to regress—is made not by an entire culture, but by one individual at a time.

Amanda Kitchen, and the five other women you are about to meet, all experienced the crisis of Power Failure as they approached the top they had so determinedly courted. Some of them, Amanda is one, grew through—and because of—the very real self-examination the crisis induced. Others chose to look away, at someone, or somewhere else, rather than within themselves.

For some of them, this crisis marked the end of their corporate careers; they would never again be offered positions of legitimate and far-reaching power.

For others, the crisis of Power Failure was merely a catalyst to examine the hidden expectations and underlying assumptions that had caused them to reject the very thing they had once so wholeheartedly sought. These two groups are representative of the ambitious career women I encounter.

Most, if not all, female corporate climbers have the seeds of sabotage within them. Some will undoubtedly reach the crisis and never recover. Others will learn from the crisis, and once again seek power, however long and painstaking a process that might be.

It is my fervent hope in writing this that the awareness of this phenomenon and its underlying causes will help women understand their internal motivations *before* they are in crisis. I also hope that women who *have* suffered Power Failure will see that there is a way out of the anger and confusion, and will be on their way to owning their own power.

The greatest hopeful message of this book—and it is where we differ significantly from many recent assessments of the problem—is that the changes can come from *within* women themselves. Executive women are not dependent on the proclamations made by the men at the top of their corporations. They can begin to alter the definitions of work and power, broaden the values inherent in corporate life, move toward Lifeplace.

Most of all, I hope this book is one step toward Lifeplace: An integrated "work" and "personal" world where members of *both* sexes make policy, where leaders of *both* genders bring their values to our institutions, our culture, our lives.

MARIA STOLLENWERK

■

She traded corporate life for corporate wife.

W HEN THE desk clerk at New York's Hotel Pierre handed me only two messages that Thursday morning in August, I was grateful.

It had been a long and challenging trip. We were in the middle of two significant searches during a month when most people are vacationing. Still, it is somewhat easier to relocate executives before September, when their children go back to school. By late October, many people stand to lose major year-end bonuses if they move before January.

So it was August in New York, and I hadn't been home in two and a half weeks. I'd been to Minneapolis, Kansas City, San Francisco, and Boston, but I hadn't been home.

I planned to return my two calls, to Maria Stollenwerk and to my office, check out, and be on a two o'clock plane.

I hadn't counted on the urgency I heard in Maria's voice.

"BarBara, would you be able to meet with me today?" There was an uncharacteristic plea in her tone. I was accustomed to Maria making pronouncements, rarely asking questions, never asking favors.

"I have to be on a plane at two o'clock," I told her. "Let's talk over the phone tomorrow."

"No, it must be today," she answered, "in person." This was sounding more like the Maria I knew.

"We'll have to have an early lunch," I told her.

"Lunch is out of the question for me, BarBara. I'm speaking at a symposium for women in communications."

I chuckled. "Maria, you're quite the joiner. Where do you find the time?"

She didn't laugh with me. "Someone has to do these things, BarBara. It's my duty to repay what I have learned."

Yes, I had temporarily forgotten, not having spoken with Maria in nearly two years. This was how she spoke about her life—with words like "duty," "someone has to," "obligation," "repay."

We agreed to meet at ten o'clock for breakfast at my hotel.

A CLASSIC CASE

I have described Amanda Kitchen's Power Failure as a complex case. She is a contemporary woman who "had it all" and was offered more.

How did we even get to a point where Amanda could be offered such a powerful opportunity, with such a smorgasbord of life options?

To understand the patriarchal culture we have all grown up with, let us review the case of one of the first "going straight for the top" executives of the seventies: Maria Stollenwerk. Hers is a classic case of the all-or-nothing orientation many women executives carried with them into their careers.

Maria's life choices grew directly out of our polarized culture.

■ ■ ■

OUR POLARIZED CULTURE

In his landmark techno-psycho-socio-economic-political thesis *The Third Wave,* Alvin Toffler describes the industrial-based society that has structured our civilization since the eighteenth century. In contrast to the land-based agricultural society (in Toffler's parlance, the First Wave) that preceded it, this Second Wave cultural organization required clearly defined roles, a highly specialized division of labor, and a mass culture. We ceased to have a "life," and began to have a "work life" and a "home life." The stronger the Second Wave culture grew, the more the tasks, responsibilities, and mental requirements of work and war were relegated to men while the tasks and emotional needs of the home became the province of women. In his subchapter entitled *The Sexual Split,* Toffler presents this view of men and women in the Second Wave:

> The same giant wedge that split producer from consumer in Second Wave societies also split work into two kinds. This had an enormous impact on family life, sexual roles, and on our inner lives as individuals.
>
> One of the most common sexual stereotypes in industrial society defines men as "objective" and women as "subjective." If there is a kernel of truth here, it probably lies not in some fixed biological reality but in the psychological effects of the invisible wedge.
>
> In First Wave societies most work was performed in the fields or in the home, with the entire household toiling together as an economic unit and with most production designed for consumption within the village or manor. Work life and home life were fused and intermingled . . . most workers performed a variety of tasks, swapping and shifting

roles as demanded by the season, by sickness, or by choice. The pre-industrial division of labor was very primitive.

Industrialization and a mass culture absolutely divided love from work, home from factory or office, situational "objectivity" from relational "subjectivity." It further divided men and women. Rather than people "swapping and shifting roles as demanded by the season, by sickness, or by choice," tasks and functions—and internal constructs—were determined first and foremost *by gender*. Personal choice and individual strengths and proclivities were overshadowed by whether one was male or female.

For women currently in the American work force, this is the culture we inherited. Unlike the First Wave society before it, jobs were specialized and segmented. "Jack-of-all-trades" became a pejorative term rather than an acknowledgment of the varied competencies of a single individual. In "indust-reality," to borrow Toffler's colorful terminology, someone could be a farmer *or* a shoemaker—not both.

Thus, when women began to enter the corporate world, there seemed to be only two options—career or marriage. Many, many women, now in their late thirties and forties, have said to me, "I wasn't going to be just a housewife, so I decided not to get married. Instead, I chose a career."

Instead. One or the other. In a world characterized by strict divisions of labor, people may consider switching roles (or choosing roles), but rarely do they consider combining them.

And so it has been with the women who pioneered corporate life in the seventies. With the newly minted feminist doctrine and a clear picture in their heads of the dreary alternative, they chose work over love, career over family, situational-objectivism over relational-subjectivism. They made an all-out either/or decision.

■　■　■

PENDULUM SWINGS

Women made this total choice of career "instead of," then expected their work to completely compensate for their sacrifice. If their work failed to do so—failed to bring them rip-roaring success *and* a sense of personal fulfillment—they often concluded that they were wrong. That, after all, it *was* the other alternative—home, family, a supportive role—that would provide fulfillment. Then they might abdicate the work world entirely for the other. Many, many women's lives today seem characterized by these wild pendulum swings between roles.

THE LOSS OF LOVE

Dr. Matina Horner, in the course of obtaining her doctorate in psychology—which would ultimately immerse her in the developing field of female psychology—first discovered in women anxieties and dreads when anticipating success. She called this the "fear of success."

At the University of Michigan in the late sixties, Dr. Horner used a method called "projective story completion" to uncover the subconscious attitudes in a sampling of male and female undergraduates. They were provided with the opening sentence of a story. The completion was up to them to write. The line was "At the end of first term finals Anne finds herself at the top of her medical school class." This was the sentence provided to the women students. The men students had the identical sentence except "Anne" was replaced by "John." Ninety percent of Dr. Horner's male respondents eagerly defined the benefits of "John's" success and projected his future rewards and happiness.

The women, however, found nothing but problems for

"Anne." She would have a life of isolation and profound unhappiness if she insisted on flaunting her academic successes. It is almost impossible to exaggerate the degree of contempt in which "Anne" was held. "Anne" was viewed as abnormal to the point that bizarre treatment such as beating her and maiming her for life is justified by her peers. One of the kindest of the story completions suggested that "Anne" cover her brilliance and help "Carl" in the hope that he will succeed and be grateful enough to marry her and then she could "concentrate on raising [Carl's] children."

Few were that benign.

Most equated success with the loss of love.

Thus, given our gender-polarized culture, and women's fear of success, Power Failure would seem virtually inevitable. Still, every woman who risks her past teachings to forge a new place brings the pendulum closer to an integrated center. Currently, the depth of their confusion is evidenced by the number of women who don't "go the distance."

SYMBOLS OF POWER

Maria Stollenwerk was one such woman. She stated she wanted power. She had the background and ability to get it. She was offered it. And she turned it down.

I had first heard of Maria Stollenwerk when she was in brand management at Childers, the unquestioned leader in packaged-goods marketing. She was one of the first women to occupy such a position, and the trade press wrote a blurb on her.

"Cum laude at Harvard, Wharton MBA. Has already dramatically improved market share on a slipping brand."

She had been campaigning to get assigned to one of the great success brands—the brands upon which present management had built their careers—but to no avail. It was during this period in her career that she called me for the first time and told me of her intentions to enter the world of advertising.

She wanted my help.

"Mrs. Bools," she began.

"Please, call me BarBara. When I hear 'Mrs. Bools' I think of my husband's mother."

"Very well, BarBara," she said with a certain degree of discomfort. Maria was a very formal and correct individual. We talked at length about her achievements and her résumé. She stated her aspirations: "I want to be in top management at a company that is considered the best in its field. Indications are that the promotions necessary to achieve that at Childers will not be forthcoming. Therefore, I have decided to maximize my options by joining English and Crenshaw."

I deciphered this MBA-speak to mean Maria had topped out at Childers and was assuming she could get a job at English and Crenshaw. She was correct in believing that a résumé with Harvard, Wharton, and Childers would be a clear door-opener.

I was concerned by her stated goal, however. It seemed to express a desire for success rather than for power. I asked her what she would like to *do* or change should she get into a top policy-making post. I got the impression she had never considered this.

"Maintain profits, of course," she said with a hint of annoyance. "Ensure the company's reputation and stature in the field. Repay what I have learned."

In the course of our initial conversation, it struck me that Maria was much more concerned with the symbols of power rather than with the exercise of power. She didn't strike me as a person who owned her own power, or who would take risks to express her ideas. This was often true of women executives, however, and Maria had it together better than most.

Her track record was very strong, for one thing, and her assumptive manner was impressive. She seemed to be a woman who knew what she wanted and was accustomed to getting it.

ENGLISH AND CRENSHAW'S CHAUVINISTIC CARROT

I believed, as she did, that she had a good chance at getting into English and Crenshaw, but I advised against it.

"Maria, you have an analytical mind. Let me present you some empirical data about English and Crenshaw. To date, there has never been a woman promoted beyond the level of senior account supervisor, and I can tell you that some have been passed up by less qualified men."

"I've persevered against stiff competition before, BarBara."

"I know you have, Maria. And you are very effective at your work. You may do very well at English and Crenshaw, should you get in. I will certainly present you there. But let me give you some more information. Last year we interviewed every one of English and Crenshaw's most promising female executives. *Every one* of the twelve has been promised the next promotion into general management."

The laws of statistics—if not just simple mathematics—would prove it was impossible for a dozen individual women to be "the next promotion into upper management." Nevertheless, that's what they all had been told and they all wanted to believe it, even though some of them knew of the promises made to their peers. Promises that could only be lies unless you don't want to see the truth.

"In my opinion, Maria," I continued, "English and Crenshaw is a very comfortable male-dominated bastion. Very clubby and very political. They get women's labor and hold out the carrot of success without ever having to share any legitimate power. I believe there is little chance for a woman to get to the top there in the near future. I recommend you also interview at a couple of other agencies. David Carr & Partners is doing some innovative things, and its top management is much less rigid. Storm & Goldman is virtually the same size as English and Crenshaw, and has been picking up new business at a good clip this year. If you really want to reach top management, I suggest either of those."

SOMETHING TO PROVE

Maria accepted the wisdom of my suggestions but didn't take it to heart. She clung to the idea of reaching the top of only the unquestioned best company. She was still nursing her disappointment at not being assigned to one of the fast-track brands at Childers, and seemed to have something to prove.

Prove to whom, I wondered. Maria's professional veneer was very thick, and finding out anything about her beyond the pat answers was difficult.

Exceptional as she was, it nonetheless took three months for Maria to go through the interviewing process, and in that time I gained some insights into her family history and motivations.

BORN INTO PATRIARCHY

Maria Stollenwerk was born in Czechoslovakia, into a classic Old World patriarchal family. Her father was a physician of some renown, and the undeniable head of the family. Her mother was submissive and powerless.

In order to escape the restrictions and political climate of their homeland, the family emigrated to Canada when Maria was a young child. Her father never again attained the standing he had had in Europe, and it was many years before he learned the language and was re-educated sufficiently to qualify for his license. Maria recounted to me once his disdain that her mother never became proficient in either English or French, and was comfortable only in a community of Czechs.

Her father was not. He drove all his children to excel by the standards of their new land. He was determined to earn enough money to send all the children to Ivy League universities.

LOVE, APPROVAL, AND SECURITY

Maria, as the oldest, felt the need to validate her father's struggle with her own success, and also be a role model for the other children. In *The Cinderella Complex,* Colette Dowling quotes a Marjorie Lozoff study done at Stanford that suggests that even the most conspicuously able women are seeking success not for its own sake, but for the sake of approval:

> In her study of "able college women," Marjorie Lozoff ferreted out a group of what she called "supercompetents." "... The fathers of the 'supercompetents,'" says Lozoff, "were aloof, self-disciplined and perfectionistic. Their demand for perfection from their daughters frequently had a narcissistic tinge to it. The young women seemed hesitant to rebel against their father's requests because of concern about the withdrawal of what little love they received."

Colette Dowling reports on this same theme many times. She also tells us that:

> Many psychologists have noted that girls are involved in achievement mainly as a way of securing

love and approval, whereas boys are involved in
achievement—or mastery—mainly for its own sake.

It was difficult, on the surface, to view Maria Stollenwerk as
someone who might be seeking love and approval. She
showed no warmth, no humor. She was all business. I did,
however, sense her strong desire for security. She spoke as
though only the perfect résumé could protect her. Only *that*
would be "enough," somehow, to keep whatever she was
afraid of at bay.

ESCAPING SUBORDINATION

In her recent book about professional women in finance, *The
Third Sex,* anthropologist Patricia McBroom provides many
telling insights about the psychological factors inherent in
high-achieving women from patriarchal families:

> The description these . . . women gave of their
> parents resemble the traditional European-Ameri-
> can patriarchal family, in which the father's will
> prevails and the mother is clearly subordinate,
> sometimes willingly, sometimes not.

McBroom reports that these women choose careers—and
choose against having children—to protect themselves from
subordination and psychological abuse. The "daughters of
patriarchy" tell of their mothers being put down, yelled at, not
taken seriously, dictated to about everything. McBroom
states:

> The feminine images they grew up with at the most
> intimate level are ones of being dominated and
> even degraded. Their defense against falling into

the same state is to walk a wide circle around maternity. Motherhood represents a loss of power. Financial independence represents the solution. These
women really believe they cannot do both; and psychologically, they can't. The issues of power and
status stand in the way. If they were to have children, they would have to work through and reject
the internal messages telling them that motherhood
imposes a state of inferiority, or else fall victim to
the same subordinated status.

McBroom describes a further influence at work in some of the
patriarchal families:

The men took over responsibility for shaping their
daughters' lives toward career values that devalued
feminine roles. The father's influence was simply
overwhelming. It was his home, his standards, his
values. Often, it seemed as if the daughters in these
families were more identified with their fathers than
with their mothers. They saw themselves as being
not like their mothers.

So we have a neat dynamic at work: Succeed to please father.
Succeed to not end up like mother.

LACKING PERSONAL POWER

This dual-edged sword is a powerful motivator for many
women. In *Secrets of a Corporate Headhunter,* John Wareham
profiles what he terms "The Amazing Female Executive—the
Amazex":

The Amazex is the eldest or only child or the only daughter, and she thus has a strong positive identi- fication with her father, accepting his values and becoming, in effect, his emotional clone. This was true in above 78 percent of all cases where women had powerful line management positions.

While this type of upbringing propels certain career women *close to* the top, it may not be enough to get them *to* the top. Why? Because it lacks personal power, and the desire to ex- press one's ideas and convictions for their own sake. In these absolutely polarized roles, women like Maria Stollenwerk can find no way to integrate their selves on a deep level.

However independent and self-assured she appeared, Maria was still acting out of a deep relationalism.

HER MIND WAS SET

Maria was offered positions by all three agencies: David Carr & Partners, Storm & Goldman, and English and Crenshaw. I advised her to take the Storm & Goldman offer, which would put her on an exciting piece of new business, and would enable her to do her own hiring and build the client/agency relationship from scratch. The DC & Partners offer was also excellent—terrific money, good title, and lots of authority.

But Maria had her mind set on English and Crenshaw. They offered her a position equal to that held by all of the other twelve women who were management hopefuls. Maria was comfortable with high-powered men of authority who de- manded absolute adherence to rules and standards—a descrip- tion that fit English and Crenshaw's management trio to a tee. Counter to my recommendation, she accepted the English and Crenshaw offer on the spot, and started her new job confident that she would be the one to break through. She believed her "perfect" credentials would ensure her success.

THE TICKET

Maria was not alone in her trust of the "perfect" credentials. In her 1985 book *Women Like Us,* Liz Roman Gallese looks at the lives of Harvard MBA women after nearly ten years in the business world. Gallese believes this group "had the first chance to make it to the top." These women seemed to have hit a wall of "Is this all there is?"

> I had noticed this pattern, whatever it was—desperation, ennui, a sense of disappointment about what it is all about—among many of the women in the class of 1975 at the Harvard Business School, and I was intrigued. So many of them had emphasized that they had gone to the Business School for what they called "The Ticket."
>
> Yet these women seemed disappointed, and profoundly so. They seemed quietly surprised that their degree wasn't a ticket to nirvana, but rather to a way of life that could be as difficult as it was rewarding, that came with demands as well as privileges.

When she joined English and Crenshaw, Maria had not yet hit this point of "desperation, ennui, a sense of disappointment." Actually, she was enlivened by her new career in advertising. However, she was decidedly not ready to accept that her credentials had purchased only her entrée into "a way of life that could be as difficult as it was rewarding" (the life that men have always faced). Rather, Maria was still hanging on to the idea that one could win by highly structured and stated rules. Looking back, I suspect that's why my advice about Storm &

Goldman or David Carr & Partners fell on deaf ears. Maria would choose only what *she* saw as the "best" company, the "best" schools, and wanted life to be as spelled out as possible.

In this respect, she was very like many of the women who embarked on corporate careers in the seventies. Very like the Harvard MBAs Gallese calls *"Women Like Us."* Women who, from the vantage point of the late 1980s, got involved but didn't get to the top.

CLOSE, BUT NO CIGAR

Maria was also very much like the pack of women management hopefuls at English and Crenshaw in many respects. What characterized them all, Maria included, was their absolute professional demeanor—their desire to assimilate "like men" into a set corporate culture.

Maria was *unlike* the other women at English and Crenshaw in one very important respect. When it came to the *work itself*—not her credentials, or the politics, but how to build a brand—she was a superior performer. Somehow, she let loose her usual "do-what's-expected" attitude, and was strategic, dynamic, and unexpected. At Childers, and at English and Crenshaw, her brands outstripped the competition. (Additionally, some promotional and new product introduction techniques that are widespread today were her innovations in the seventies.)

This very performance *did* separate her from the pack. Maria Stollenwerk was the first female executive at English and Crenshaw to break through. She was the first female vice-president, the first management supervisor, the first female on the cover of their glossy systemwide in-house magazine.

Close, but no cigar. In order to achieve this promotion, however, she had to accept, from the men in power, a low-profile, low-power account that had no chance of growing in size or stature. It was a comfortable, "maintenance" account, where Maria's strategic brilliance would be wasted.

(Interestingly, four of the twelve women who were Maria's peers, and whom she passed up, were pregnant within the year. Six—fully half—are no longer in the business at all.)

In addition, English and Crenshaw kept Maria's schedule full of public appearances and PR appointments.

She had become a token.

REALITY VS. PERCEPTION

As a token, Maria's very visibility only added to the growing media and cultural expectations of women's acceptance in the corporate world, and their growing power therein.

Maria (and often the media) missed an important truth— problems are opportunities. Maria needed to be challenged, to be someplace where her background and skills overrode her gender. At English and Crenshaw—accustomed to people with top credentials and MBAs from the best schools—Maria's gender was still the issue. The men in this male-dominated bastion did not covet the idea of a woman outshining them, so English and Crenshaw effectively sidelined her despite her stellar performance, and she was unable to exercise *her leadership value* within English and Crenshaw's comfortable top management.

TWICE BURNED

When she called me for breakfast that August morning in New York, she realized she had been sidelined and tokenized a second time. Maria seemed finally ready to listen to my

advice about the marketplace and her legitimate opportunities. She reiterated her burning ambition to reach The Top.

A GREAT OPPORTUNITY

It was a recession year, and the advertising business was hurting. I thought Maria's brand-building talents could earn her
real power back on the corporate side. We agreed she would
stay on the English and Crenshaw treadmill until the right
thing came along.

Just two months later one of my clients introduced me to the
head of Faraday Farms.

Faraday Farms is one of the leading meat-packing companies that had started with beef and pork and moved into
poultry as the tastes of the country moved in that direction.
What had started as little more than a sausagemaker had
grown to a mammoth food processor with plants all over the
country. Many of these plants had sprung up to be close to the
farms that Faraday bought out during the Depression. (For the
longest time "Faraday Farms" had been uttered with anger
and hatred. People have short memories, however, and today
a word like "farms" sounds bucolic and smacks of something
homemade and wholesome.) Faraday Farms had become a
resounding success and was riding the crest of America's redis-
covery of chicken and turkey and its disenchantment with red
meat.

The principals at Faraday Farms had all come up through
the ranks of sales and really didn't grasp the intricacies and
nuances of strategic marketing. They knew only that there was
something going on out there that worked and they wanted
to get in on more of it.

I suggested Maria to them. She could establish a brand
managment system, increase sales, gain the needed visibility

for their brands, capitalize on the changes in the country, and lead them right to the top. The company was not vulnerable to takeover. The principals were in their sixties, and there was no heir apparent. It was a great opportunity for Maria.

They liked her. She liked them. In fact, they loved her. They loved her savvy and her obvious brilliance. The unquestioned inevitability of her suggestions. They weren't sure what they didn't possess, but they knew they didn't possess it. Maria did. And they knew that, too. They were taken with her talents and credentials. The position had another nice little twist to it. Faraday Farms competed head-on with a large division of one of English and Crenshaw's cornerstone accounts. Maria would have the opportunity to demonstrate her abilities *outside* English and Crenshaw in a way that had never been possible from within.

It could have been a showcase for Maria: the opportunity to take one of America's oldest companies and virtually make it over into a stunningly successful marketer.

POWER FAILURE

But she hesitated. This was a side to Maria I hadn't seen before. Previously, her only direction had been forward, and then at a never-fast-enough pace. Now, for the first time, there was a self-imposed pause.

Maria's hesitation prompted the men from Faraday Farms to go into full courtship mode, which in their case, with their frame of reference, meant inundating Maria with samples of the specialties of Faraday Farms. To keep my interest (which wasn't waning) and support (which never faltered), I, too, was put on the list. Over the next two weeks there were frequent deliveries of Faraday Farms's finest. Either Maria was going to accept the job or together we would seriously have to consider opening a delicatessen. Neither happened.

I called Maria one day after the delivery of some smoked turkey breast to see if she had sorted things out.

Her response left no doubt.

"I don't want anything else from that slaughterhouse, Bar-Bara. Can't you make them stop?"

Slaughterhouse, I thought. That was a harsh attack, in no way warranted. Where was this vindictive change of heart coming from?

I decided to fly back to New York to talk with Maria face to face. I spoke with her for hours in an attempt to uncover the difficulty.

WHAT IT WASN'T

I became convinced the problem was not inherent in the offer itself, the location, the personalities, or the title or money or authority. I thought perhaps Maria was fearful of her ability to develop a marketing and brand management system from scratch rather than step into an existing one. Our conversation revealed that Maria was *not* afraid of that. It was the most exciting aspect of the job for her—to develop and build unfettered by pre-existing conditions. She welcomed that challenge. No, the problem wasn't anything fixable.

WHAT IT WAS

Only the "best" schools, the "best" companies would validate Maria's father's life-long struggle. Though she never used those words, that was the single issue she kept dancing around and returning to. She was working to achieve a top spot at a top company for *his* approval, for *his* security and peace of mind. Her concern was that her father wouldn't see the opportunity and excitement in a challenge like Faraday Farms; he would see only that she hadn't "made it" in a top company. It wouldn't be "good enough for Papa." Her fear was his fear that his European children would never be totally accepted, totally privileged, totally safe.

She was operating out of a deep relationalism.

AN AGGRESSIVE YOUNG MAN

Maria became so frozen at the prospect of violating the approved family script that she never officially turned down the Faraday Farms offer. Ultimately, I withdrew her as a candidate. We filled the position within a month with an aggressive young man who *also* had an Ivy League and Childers résumé. After his initial interview he quickly developed a plan to organize a marketing system at Faraday, and asked to present his "rough outline" to the board. He and his wife entertained two of the principals and their wives with a meal full of Faraday Farms meats. Naturally enough, this candidate's enthusiasm and love of their company caused Faraday to love him back. Maria's misunderstood reluctance—and Maria—were soon forgotten.

"A POWERFUL MAN"

I thought Maria needed a little time to accept what had happened and to sort things out. I planned to talk with her again in a few months and determine whether she had become ready to entertain a less-than-"best" company—whether she would be able to look at an opportunity without other people's expectations in the way.

But Maria made my efforts unnecessary.

Shortly afterward she called to say she had resigned from English and Crenshaw and married Thomas Cernek. He was nearly the age of her father. In fact, he had befriended her father when the Stollenwerks first arrived in Canada. Thomas Cernek had helped Maria's father re-establish himself and qualify for the exams that would allow him to practice medicine in his new country. Thomas Cernek was an extremely generous man. He was also an extremely wealthy man, purported to be one of the richest in the northern hemisphere. Perhaps most important of all, he was the chairman of New York's most prestigious international bank. In a word, the *best*. He had first asked Maria's father for the privilege of marrying Maria when she graduated from her Catholic girls' school. That's how it had been done in the old country. But Maria had been accepted on full scholarship to Harvard, and besides, she had things to do. Things she had to do for her father.

Maria had once told me that she had fallen head-over-heels in love while at Harvard. "I had so much to do first," she had said. "I had to be free to accept opportunities unfettered. I wasn't ready to get married."

Apparently, she got ready.

"You must be very excited," I said to Maria, "to be in love again." Her answer was, "He's a powerful man." Then she changed the subject.

For profoundly personal reasons she demanded security. From the time she was a child, security was something that could be bought and sold and was very fragile. Her résumé was her security and, by her standards, it could not, would not, include a "slaughterhouse." She still carried her father's message that they were strangers in a strange land. However, she misread her real options. For all of her intelligence she never saw what was really happening all around her. She saw only what had happened to her father.

■   ■   ■

POWER BY ASSOCIATION

Maria had made another trade-off. This time she traded corporate life to become a corporate wife.

In *Secrets of a Corporate Headhunter,* John Wareham delivers a chilling Ralph Nader quote:

> Young wives are the leading asset of corporate power. . . . They want society to see that they have exchanged themselves for something of value.

This seemed to be true of Maria. She had sought power and status *for her father* and for external expectations. Thus, when that didn't come easily, she was willing to substitute power by association (her husband's power and status). Had she desired power for the joy of expressing her own beliefs, she would not have considered getting it vicariously.

THE SEEDS OF POWER FAILURE

How true this is of women who embarked upon corporate careers in the seventies! Operating out of relationalism, seeking mastery not for its own sake, but for the sake of approval, the seeds of their Power Failure are in them long before they may actually say "no" to a top post. Consider this, from Jean Baker Miller's *Toward a New Psychology of Women:*

> Psychological troubles are the worst kind of slavery—one becomes enlisted in creating one's own enslavement—one uses so much of one's own energies to create one's own defeat.
>
> All forms of oppression encourage people to enlist in their own enslavement.

Oppression in our culture has encouraged women to put other people's expectations *first*—before the reality of the market-place, before the assessment of one's own talents and abilities, before the need for mastery and self-determination. It is a *relational* rather than *situational* orientation.

It appears, to the casual observer, that Maria "has it all." She does indeed have the breathtaking duplex on Park Avenue, the stunning retreats in Bermuda and Vail.

She shops, does lunch, has catered dinners for twelve, and drinks too much.

THE CONSEQUENCES OF POWER FAILURE

In addition to the individual stories I relate here, everyone knows of a promising woman executive who, for one reason or another, fell off the fast track. One woman at a time, their choices are understandable:

- "She wanted to spend more time with her children."
- "She prefers public relations to line management."
- "Her company wanted to transfer her but her husband's practice is really booming."

But there are those of us—recruiters, human resource directors, business reporters, sociologists—who face executive women's choices in the aggregate.

Other recruiters have commented:

- "It doesn't pay to call women."
- "Women go along to a point, then they cop out for no good reason, and I look bad to my client."
- "If I've got a few months to fill a position, I'll call on women. Hell, *I'm* a woman! But if the job needs to be done fast, forget it."

- "I hate it when the CEO says, 'A woman would be good here.' It's like saying, 'We don't have any women in-house we can promote, so find us one outside.' But he doesn't realize there are none outside!"
- "If the job means relocation, there won't be a woman on my call list. My call only makes them uncomfortable."

Most human resource people echo the sentiments of this Bools & Associates client, the director of human resources of a Fortune 500 company:

- "We really need some women in the top management ranks. In the last two re-alignments, there were a few women who had enough skill and experience, but they're missing something."

Or *this* Bools & Associates client:

- "In their mid-thirties the women get ambivalent, undecided about their careers. Or else they don't see the big picture, what their work means for the whole company. Something seems to go out of them, and they just tread water."

Business Week, June 22, 1987, tells us this about the top 100 corporate women whom they profiled in 1976,

No CEOs emerged from the pioneering group. . . . In all, only five women are working in the kinds of line jobs considered crucial for a shot at senior executive positions.

Ann Morrison, Randall White, and Ellen Van Velsor of The Center for Creative Leadership, in their recent book, *Breaking the Glass Ceiling,* ask the question "Can Women Reach the Top of America's Largest Corporations?" In their concluding chapter, they answer this question.

> We expect to see no more than a handful of women reach the senior management level of Fortune 100–sized corporations within the next two decades.

They believe that women will not reach the "highest levels of major corporations for at least another generation."

The authors continue: "We predict that women will take top management posts within the next 50 years."

That will be the year 2038.

As I write this, many women—like Maria Stollenwerk—no longer work.

Unlike Maria Stollenwerk, Vicki Dennison was not a woman who sat still, would never be "a woman who waits." Vicki was determined to move forward at an ever-accelerating pace even if she had no idea where that would take her. Or why the journey was not to be denied.

VICKI DENNISON

■

They both played the game, but he played to win.

T HE VERY first time I met Vicki Dennison she announced that she wanted power.

"BarBara, I want power. Lots of power. I'm an Army brat and I know all about power: what life is like with it—and without it. Do you know the Sophie Tucker saying 'I've been rich and I've been poor. Rich is better'?"

I was surprised she even knew who Sophie Tucker was, let alone could quote her. I gathered that the "rich is better" was a stand-in for "power is better." I'd buy that. Vicki did, obviously.

Here was this tiny (barely five feet tall) gamine, no, make that "waif"—standing there with all the fire and conviction of an evangelist with a mission. "And communication is power, and advertising is communication on an enormous scale." And then, after barely a pause, "And I love advertising."

She said it as if she had just discovered it. The way some teenagers talk about love as if they had just invented it. Maybe she had. Vicki had an "invented" quality about her, and she wanted to put her stamp on everything she touched. She was a free spirit with short, shaggy, almost black hair framing remarkable green eyes and a full sensuous mouth that erupted often with her wry, unpredictable humor. She designed her own clothes and virtually everything she wore had that one-of-a-kind quality that matched her own one-of-a-kind quality. Although she never went over the edge in her outrageousness, she did manage to push it for all it was worth.

"THIS TIME IT'LL ONLY GET BETTER"

Nothing about her seemed conventional or conformist. Even her art education and background was not from the "right" schools—the ones who channel the best and the brightest into the business—but from the Sorbonne. As an Army brat she had tasted the life of a nomad and decided it was for her. Each of the frequent moves in her past had held out the promise so often stated by her mother: "This time it'll only get better. You'll see." It was a belief system that Vicki would carry with her.

She started her career at Paris *Vogue* and used that experience to bring her to the States. She brought with her the slightest difficult-to-place European accent which only added to her uniqueness and undeniable charm. She told me she had quickly become bored with fashion's temperaments and tears, its pretenders and predators. So she had done what she knew to do to get a fresh start, to "make it better"—she moved. She moved to L.A.—for someone trying to escape "pretenders and predators," there's an irony here—and worked on car and motorcycle magazines.

It was only a short time before she gravitated to a small, exciting agency that was doing sensational advertising and getting a sudden and very much deserved reputation as the hottest young shop in the country.

She was a natural at advertising. She loved it. It loved her.

Whenever the agency was profiled, Vicki was photographed. Vicki was winning awards. Vicki's enthusiasm made great editorial copy in the trade magazines. Vicki became the new star rising in the west.

"GOING TO THE TOP"

It was on a trip to L.A. that I first met her. The rumors, the publicity, were all true, but not nearly true enough. In person, Vicki was a little more than I had been expecting. Her life was full and exciting. She loved the power she was beginning to experience and the control she was beginning to exercise. This was when she first told me how much she wanted that power and everything that came with the package. She was single and "going right to the top of the business." She had "no desire to tie myself down." Everything was too good "to complicate it with a serious relationship." She stated clear choices. Nothing was going to get in her way.

At photographer Jon Mack's party one night, Vicki was clearly the center of attention. She couldn't help but revel in it—most of the endless stream of transparencies projected on huge screens were of her. (Mack, on assignment to "capture" the essence of the agency where Vicki worked, was instead captured by Vicki, and the results were being displayed with rock music accompaniment on three of his studio walls.)

In the midst of that night where she was clearly a star, a tall, thin, intense man took her arm, spoke to her in impeccable French, and told her she was behaving badly and that he was taking her out of there. She allowed herself to be led away without looking back.

Brian had entered her life.

■   ■   ■

EVERYTHING SHE DIDN'T NEED

Brian was everything Vicki didn't need: disruptive, demanding, divorced. He was also Vietnamese by birth, very elegant, and at ease in any situation.

He appealed to that part of Vicki that sought the surprising adventure. If it was a little unconventional and outrageous, well, that was all the better.

Within days Brian moved in with her. They were inseparable. They were both associate creative directors, Vicki at the brilliant agency where she was making her mark, and Brian at a huge plodding agency where he had long been a good, competent writer acknowledged for his beguiling headlines. To contrast them, he was an excellent manager and very professional; Vicki's work was thrilling. They maintained their professional and personal status throughout the next year. Brian's ex-wife remarried and moved with her new husband to New York. She took with her the son and daughter she and Brian had had together. Brian hated the 3,000-mile separation from his kids. Most of all, he hated that they were being raised by another man. He managed to bid most of his commercial productions with New York directors. He was so glib that he easily convinced everyone involved that a shoot could be accomplished only by a particular director, who happened to be in New York. (Writers and art directors in inclement climates have been doing this for years to get to L.A.: "We open on a palm tree and pan down to the product in the sand and then . . ." I guess it was inevitable that someone would reverse the procedure.) The occasional trips to New York still weren't satisfactory for Brian.

                              ■   ■   ■

DISCUSSING THEIR PROSPECTS

Eventually, he told Vicki it was time to move east.

That was great with her: Moving was second nature to her and she did it comfortably and easily. She loved the excitement and challenge of new places. She was ready to move. She was always ready to move. And it would always be up.

I met with both of them in Los Angeles. At first, I was surprised by Brian; I guess I had expected someone more like Vicki. He was nothing like her at all, and gave new meaning to the cliché about opposites attracting. He was at least a foot taller than she was. He was reserved. Downright still. And humorless. Nevertheless, Vicki had enough enthusiasm and energy and bounce for both of them. Throughout a long, rambling afternoon, we discussed their prospects and how to best go about an impending move.

THE PERFECT OPENING

They wanted a small, creative market in the East. Their first city of choice was Boston, and they asked me about opportunities there. I concurred that Boston was an ideal market for them. It was growing, and coming into its own, and the potential for them was explosive.

I made it clear to them they would probably have to be separated for upward of a few months, because surely one would get a job offer before the other. They both agreed. Vicki and Brian assured me they were savvy about opportunities and location and were confident that they would *both* land better positions in Boston, no matter who went first. They reiterated their individual desires to go all the way to the top. I was hearing it for the first time from Brian. I had never heard anything less from Vicki.

Although at the time none of our Boston clients had needs at Vicki's and Brian's level, my good clients count on me to keep them aware of opportunities to attract special people. Both Brian and Vicki were special in different ways: Either one would be an asset to a creative department.

About a month later the president of Boston's hottest agency called me and wanted to arrange to meet both Brian and Vicki. They had a particular opening that would be perfect for Vicki. They were on the threshold of some exciting new business opportunities and wanted the additional excitement they believed Vicki could add. There might also be something for Brian, but even if it didn't pan out that way with them, they could almost guarantee a position with another agency in town with which they had a particularly cooperative relationship.

[These two agencies were rarely in competition with each other because their styles and structures were very different. Each appealed to a different type of client, with very little crossover. The agency heads had a long-standing friendship and a mutual respect, which I believed could be parlayed into a strength for the Boston ad community.]

". . . I WISH THEY ALL COULD BE CALIFORNIA GIRLS"

The agency made arrangements for Vicki and Brian to fly to Boston. When the two of them stepped into Logan Airport they were greeted with huge signs saying WELCOME TO L.A. and fourteen of the agency's finest dressed in floral shirts and cutoffs and strange clothes that represented L.A. All of this was accompanied by a tape of the Beach Boys and the strains of "I wish they all could be California girls." It didn't matter that it was February in Boston. Nor did it matter that Brian was dressed in an impeccable Armani suit, didn't and *wouldn't* own a flowered shirt, and that neither Brian nor Vicki had ventured toward the beach in their entire time together. (They were too cerebral for that.) It didn't matter at all. All that mattered is that Boston—or at least the advertising community there—took them to its heart. And wanted them to stay.

That was made all the more convincing when Vicki was offered the position of creative director—one of three at the agency—a major step up for her in position, title, function, and money.

Brian was introduced to many people at three different agencies and had some very good interviews but no offers.

"I WISH THE SITUATION WERE REVERSED"

At the end of the week, tired but exhilarated, they flew back to Los Angeles. Vicki agreed to give her response before the end of the following week.

All of us at Bools & Associates were certain she could only say "yes" to the position. Numerous versions of the welcome and the other highlights of the week had been relayed to us with ever-increasing elaboration and enthusiasm. (In keeping with their personalities, Brian elaborated while Vicki enthused. Even so, Brian seemed to be getting caught up in the excitement.)

Most important, it was exactly what Vicki and Brian had said they wanted. And then some. It was the first step toward their successful relocation to Boston—the market of their choice.

Vicki called me on Monday and indicated indirectly that there were complications. This was a first for Vicki, who had always been so direct and straightforward.

"BarBara, isn't there some way that things can be speeded up for Brian?"

"I can't think of anything that would do that faster than your acceptance of the position," I answered firmly. "That's the best message you could deliver to both Brian and the advertising community in Boston about the sincerity of your commitment."

"I just wish the situation were reversed and Brian had the offer," she sighed.

I reminded her that she and Brian *had agreed* to support whomever received the first offer. She agreed with that again but said somewhat wistfully—and very uncharacteristically— "He's so proud, you know, and it will be difficult for him to appear to be following me. I'd miss him so much while we were apart."

"Vicki, if you turn this opportunity down, there may not be another available when you are ready. Are you and Brian ready to give up the Boston move at this time?"

"No, BarBara. We still want to go. I just want to be sure it's right to move first."

Once again I reminded her of their decision. "You and Brian both agreed that whoever got the first offer would move and the other would follow. Be sure to examine all the ramifications of your decision, Vicki."

She totally avoided my statement by saying, "The job is really great. I have no problems with that. It's personal. I'm not ready to make a decision. I'll call you soon."

The familiar, and unfortunately increasingly familiar, sense of foreboding surfaced in me at Vicki's remark, "It's personal," which had come to mean to me—it's relational.

I want to step momentarily away from Vicki to share some occurrences that highlight the different—and all too often, predictable—behavior of men and women: men who behave situationally, and women who behave relationally.

▪   ▪   ▪

FORTY MEN AND ONE WOMAN

I am less and less shocked by powerhouse women who, amazingly, won't even interview for positions their male counterparts are drooling over. Consider this unique executive search assignment we received from a highly respected advertising agency. It is privately held, with equity potential down the road for a few top players. They believe in minimal layers for maximum communication and were offering a truly powerful position: president/director of account services.

Normally the two positions are split in an agency. An ambitious group account director first would have to obtain the director of account services post, perform exceptionally well for five to eight years, and pray that a presidency position would open up somewhere. This very rare set of circumstances as presented to us would allow an executive to leapfrog. This was clearly a special opportunity for the right person.

We searched in ten major U.S. cities. Nationwide, the group of candidates we deemed appropriate contained approximately equal numbers of men and women, about forty each.

Of the forty men, not one man hesitated.

Only one woman even interviewed.

This unusual woman had worked with the chairman some nine years earlier and was excited by the opportunity to resume a very pleasant working relationship with a man she admired. After their meeting, she believed they would make an excellent team to run that office. She was also pleased at their clear and unquestioned acceptance of women. She agreed to take the next steps.

The next week she sheepishly announced that her husband had just received a significant promotion and she would no longer be able to consider relocation.

Executive recruiters and human resource departments consistently report difficulties in relocating women that far exceed those encountered in relocating men.

". . . AND I'D BE PRESIDENT"

One of our associates related the preceding story of a search and its outcome to a couple of young women at a party shortly after the event. One of the women, Emily, is on a very fast track at a top insurance company. She has parlayed her MBA from an excellent school into a highly visible position. Her husband, Mike, holds a similar position with another company. Emily empathized immediately with the women Bools & Associates had contacted for this particular search.

"To move clear across the country I'd have to ask not if this were good for *me,* but for both of us. Mike would have to quit his job and all—it would be a tremendous risk. I can understand not wanting the responsibility of doing that to your husband."

Emily was then asked how she felt *Mike* would respond to something like this opportunity.

"Oh, I'm sure he'd be very supportive," she answered, glancing across the room at her husband, who smiled and waved at her, "but I'd be making six figures." She took a deep breath and continued. "I mean"—her voice grew distressed and she seemed to be describing a totally unacceptable scenario—"he'd be out of work—and I'd be president."

"A HEADHUNTER CALLED TODAY, HONEY"

Emily's friend Linda spoke next. Linda is in management at a Big Eight accounting firm. She mentioned she frequently received calls from recruiters offering better-paying, higher-level opportunities, usually, for some reason, on the East Coast. She, unlike Emily, *did* go home and discuss these possibilities with her husband, who is in sales.

She was asked how she usually presented that kind of news to her husband.

Linda threw her head back and laughed in self-recognition.

"Well, I go home and say, 'A headhunter called today, honey, but I'm not so sure it's a big deal, and besides, we don't want to move to New York, do we?"

Our associate suggested to these young women that their actions, combined with those of thousands of other professional women, could well have the result that their daughters, the next generation, will enter a work world with no women at the top—that their daughters might very well believe that relocation is an option only for a man's career.

Emily and Linda smiled and had no answers. It seemed to be a new concept to each of them.

"MY WIFE'S NO PROBLEM"

Compare this attitude with that of a young male executive in his thirties, whose wife happened to be a respected vice-president of a large regional retail chain. When asked about his wife's career (in reference to his) his instant reply was, "My wife's no problem."

Another male executive, David, thirty-two, was well paid, well respected, and blocked. When we called with an out-of-town opportunity, he chuckled and said, "Not really. I couldn't entertain anything else right now because my wife's eight months pregnant. She's all set with the hospital, and her obstetrician is a gem. Her mom will help with the baby and her company is begging her to come back to work as soon as possible after the baby is born, which, incidentally, she wants very much to do." He took a deep and well-deserved breath after that, and then with mingled curiosity and growing interest, "But just for kicks, what's the job?"

When he learned the job was as a division director—the job his boss currently had—but at another company, he quickly added, "Oh, God. Maureen's gonna kill me. Let me talk to her tonight and I'll call you first thing in the morning."

He did, of course.

Two days later, they both—or, more accurately, 2.8 of them—sat in my office trying to cope with the bewildering legion of logistics necessary to execute a move at this particular time. It would mean new doctors, no job for her to return to, no nearby grandparents, selling their home, buying a new one, executing a move, shipping their cars, and it would eliminate the three-week leave *he* was planning to take when the baby was born.

Were they up to all of this?

I watched them and believed David would support whatever Maureen decided. I watched her weigh the possibilities, sigh, and straighten her shoulders in determination. Clearly, the way they understood it—or at least the way *she* understood it—David's career came first. Not knowing whether David would even get the position (there were other superb candidates vying for it), they nonetheless were on a plane two days later for a second round of interviews, this time in the city where the new job existed.

While David interviewed, Maureen spent the day with a realtor.

BACK TO VICKI

Consequently, I recognized Vicki's reluctance and waffling as the beginning of a process that usually resulted in no action taken. But taking no action is still a decision—a decision to remain in whatever situation previously existed.

THE WOLF AT THE DOOR

I called the president at the Boston agency and explained my interpretation of the situation. It certainly wasn't hopeless, but it didn't appear promising either. He reassured Vicki that Brian would surely get a good offer soon. Magnanimously, he also sent Vicki a hooded wolf parka with the explanation that it really *wasn't* L.A., that it *was* Boston and they needed her right away.

A week later she still hadn't reached a decision. The agency called her to ask that she return to Boston for further discussions. She declined—both the trip *and* the position.

She told me that she and Brian had discussed their options at length and decided to go to New York instead of Boston: Brian would be closer to his kids that way and it seemed to be a better market for both of them.

WITHOUT HESITATION

The process began all over again. Only this time Vicki was aware and honest enough to tell me up front she intended to wait until Brian got the job *he* wanted, and then she would begin her search again in earnest.

I was saddened by this and had seen the real-world repercussions this type of attitude tended to have on both women's careers and personal lives. She was fusing her career with her relationship. I called her on it. She became very defensive and made excuses, insisting that New York had more to offer them both. That was not the issue. She really never addressed the priorities: Brian's priorities.

Shortly thereafter, one of the agencies where Brian had interviewed in Boston lost their creative director. That same afternoon they called Brian direct in Los Angeles and offered him the job.

Brian accepted the position. Without hesitation. Without consulting Vicki.

She called me to see if the original offer in Boston could be reactivated. "I still have the parka, BarBara. Doesn't that mean the job is still open?"

"No, it only means you still have the parka. You turned it down. They hired someone else."

"But they wanted me!" She almost wailed it.

RULES NOT TO BE BROKEN

"No doubt. Just the same, you left them hanging. Now they've moved on."

There were no other openings in Boston that even approached her level. At the time Boston was a relatively small advertising market and she had blown her opportunity with its best agency. Worst of all, management at that agency—in its unbridled enthusiasm—had spread word all over town that Vicki would be joining them. Ultimately, they also spread the word that she had led them down the garden path and refused the position. It was not advertising's finest moment. The informed of the Boston advertising community knew she had made a bad decision. She would not be taken seriously after that. Even advertising has rules that are not to be broken.

RULES SHE BROKE

Vicki gave away power and then was surprised when Brian took it.

Vicki's actions taught Brian that she would forgo the stated contract in favor of the unspoken contract: that *his* career and *his* ego were paramount.

It also seemed, however, that part of Vicki's unspoken contract was, "I'll sacrifice for him, and he'll do right by me." Clearly, her observable behavior had only reinforced Brian's man-first-woman-second internal messages. Her demonstrable action suggested that *she* needed his career to come first, before she could advance.

Thus when Brian was presented an opportunity to further his career, he accepted it. Was he betraying Vicki? Or only acting in concert with her observable rules?

Brian tried to get her to come along, but she felt betrayed by Brian. Brian went anyway. Out of her house. Out of her life.

RUNNING AWAY

In the wake of Brian's move, Vicki dealt with her sense of loss and betrayal by regressing to a comfortable pattern from her childhood: She also moved. With a vengeance. She left the country.

Vicki joined the international division of Watson, Rand, & Crowell, a large agency always on the lookout for that rare combination of creative talent and multilingual experience. She ran away. She spent the next five years moving from one country to the next as an international trouble-shooter, essentially a hired gun. These jobs were primarily maintenance work at the time. I'm sure Vicki did that very well. But the woman who wanted to put her stamp on her industry, who wanted power in communications, must have been very frustrated by the continued sameness of her work experience, despite the *appearance* of change with every move. For there was always another troubled account or situation over the next mountain. In five years time she had nothing she could call her own.

She returned to the States, to a decent job and salary at the headquarters of Watson, Rand & Crowell in New York. She was tired of running. Maybe she was just tired. She had had five years with lots of change, lots of stress, and no forward movement.

When Brian heard she was back in the States he got in touch with her, saying he wanted to see her. He wanted to get back together. This time things would be different. He did not want to lose her from his life again. He flew to New York to see her. He was now the senior vice-president/executive creative director and offered her a job as an art director, the only position he had open in his department.

Vicki looked straight at him and said very carefully, "Let me get this straight. Five years ago you and I were both ACDs. We were at the same level in our careers."

Brian agreed.

"Now you are an ECD—a senior vice-president," she continued, "and you're offering me a job as an art director."

Again, Brian agreed.

"Brian, I can say 'fuck you' in at least six languages. Pick one."

Brian didn't understand the hostility. "It's the only opening I have right now, Vicki. You can grow."

"Go to hell, Brian."

Instead, he returned to Boston.

This was the point where she called me and asked if we could meet again. I told her I would be in New York in a couple of weeks and we could get together then. I had lost track of her and was genuinely interested in what had happened to her life.

■   ■   ■

INSIGHTS

We met for lunch. I expected her to look different, at least older. Everyone else had aged just about five years. Not Vicki. She was radiant. Lovelier than ever. And now it was all graced with an appealing gloss of maturity that nudged very carefully at the gamine. But it was still the gamine who spoke.

"Let me tell you about my tour of duty in the Foreign Legion, where the creed is 'No Questions Asked.' "

"Sounds like it would make a great movie."

"But first, some insights into my childhood."

"I love insights."

"My mother was"—she corrected herself—"*is* the most remarkable woman and the most remarkably independent woman I have ever known. I used to think she was perfect. She ran our house with military precision that matched my dad's, but she also cooked and baked like a sonofabitch, held all the Girl Scout meetings in our home, taught me to play the piano, tutored me in algebra, and made all my clothes. I was hot shit the whole time I was in school. And of course there were dozens of schools because we moved every time my dad was promoted or whatever. Mom always said, 'This time it'll be even better than before.' She saw moving as an adventure. And she was always there for me. Always."

TWO ROLE MODELS IN ONE

For the first time, Vicki took her steady gaze from my face.

"Until Rambo came home. Then Mom changed. *How* she changed. June Cleaver became Delilah. Beaver's mom became the sex goddess the minute those heavy boots hit the front porch." There was another long pause. "I've been in therapy, BarBara, trying to get a handle on things and I'm giving you the 'news update' version. You want film at eleven?''

"Are you kidding?" I replied. "Who could turn off the *Adventures of Rambo and Delilah?*"

"Okay." She laughed and continued easily. "Basically, my mother was two—count them, two—role models for me: the totally independent woman who throws it all aside to be there for 'her man' from across the seas. Get the picture? See any similarity to my behavior with Brian?''

I was a little taken aback. It all sounded so textbook, so Psychology 101. But it did fall into place.

Vicki continued. "Want to hear the capper? She's a Gemini.''

With that the two of us broke up.

Eventually, amid the laughter I did get the full story. As she called it, *The World According to Vicki.*

She was starting to understand, through therapy, what all those moves had been about.

In *Unfinished Business,* Maggie Scarf's treatise about women and depression, she tells of a depressed adolescent, Anne, who has not managed to separate, psychologically, from her parents. In her first major push to do so, Anne campaigned for the right to attend a boarding school nearly a thousand miles away from her parents.

> There are two strategies that adolescents frequently resort to when they can't quite manage to achieve that real, that inner independence—the confidence that they can care for themselves and survive on their own resources—which is psychological in nature.
>
> One strategy is that of remaining too close to the parents. . . . The other strategy is that of putting distance between oneself and one's family: going very far away from the parents in order to create the facade of an achieved independence. But in this

instance, as in the former instance, the psychological task of separation hasn't been completed.

In Vicki Dennison's family of origin, many issues of "becoming," especially her mother's need to have an independent life, were never constructively dealt with. Rather than dealing with problematic issues in the family, they perpetuated the myth that "everything will be better with the next move."

So whenever Vicki confronted an unfair situation in her own life, she was more likely to take to the road than to stand her ground and fight it out. As Maggie Scarf continues about Anne, I feel I could be reading about Vicki Dennison:

> [She] . . . denied her powerful dependency feelings, and . . . put much geographic mileage between herself and a psychological task that she'd found too difficult to confront. . . .

CONFRONTING THE ISSUES

She also told me she was ready to get on with her career, and had achieved the maturity to stick it out in one place. Once again she stated she wanted power and influence.

"And this time," she told me, "if some stud darkens my doorway, he's welcome to stay, but I'm leading my own life. The next time I move, or *don't* move, it will be wholly *my* decision. And I hope it's not for a long time."

While Vicki Dennison was still a woman who would struggle with certain issues of what it means to be "feminine," she was light years ahead of the Maria Stollenwerks of the world.

For starters, she had a mother who had demonstrated the dichotomy between independence and femininity. Vicki had lived out this conflict in her own life.

And lived through it. Vicki's greatest asset in overcoming

Power Failure was her deep commitment at this point to "stick it out" and "lead my own life."

She was also light years ahead of the Maria Stollenwerks for another reason. Maria had grown up with the system of patriarchy at the most intimate level—her *father's* unquestioned authority permeated every aspect of her family life. Vicki's family, however, was reacting to a patriarchal system *outside* their family—that of the *Army's* unquestioned authority to change every aspect of their lives. Vicki told me that she believed her mother might have had an important occupation, or some vocation, had she ever been able to stay in one place.

Which is exactly what Vicki now intended to do.

ONE MORE MOVE

She knew without my having to tell her that one more move—although not a geographic one—would be necessary. The management at Watson, Rand & Crowell had very high regard for her, but as a maintenance person. She really had not established any kind of core group there, and she certainly didn't belong to one. She was still thought of as an extremely effective hired gun. To move forward would indeed require one more move.

"STOP SENDING FLOWERS"

I advised her to sit tight until the right thing came along and then be ready for it. It was not Vicki's nature to sit and wait, but she was prepared to change those parts of her nature that no longer suited her goals.

Several months later (five months to be exact—I know because each month Vicki sent me a bouquet with a card that inevitably said, "Forget-me-not"), I received an assignment for a high-level creative position at an exciting agency. I had three strong candidates in mind, and Vicki was one of them.

I called Vicki. "Stop sending the flowers. Get ready. This is it."

RECORD SALES

Vicki topped the list, and accepted the offer without hesitation. The first commercial Vicki created at her new agency was for Deny, the Woman's Deodorant. Previously, Deny had been advertised as if it were on a level with the Salk vaccine. White-coated actors seriously described the inherent benefits and dimensions of the roller apparatus while strolling around an immense all-white laboratory busy with the hum of invention and progress. They were ordinary commercials for an ordinary product.

Vicki's commercial miraculously—but not surprisingly—combined the excitement of foreign travel with the unique independence of the American Woman. It was a breakthrough campaign that truly honored the viewer.

For three months after that, they couldn't make the stuff fast enough. They had record sales—they were clearing their warehouses. The next year Vicki won a Clio for that commercial.

BUILDING POWER

Although Vicki effectively "lost" five years of career growth, this story has a happy ending. With the shock of realizing that Brian's career had grown while hers had stagnated or regressed, Vicki learned to attend to her own situation, independent of her relationships. Vicki reaffirmed her original desire to put her stamp on her industry, and has been building both her personal and organizational power ever since.

A year after her first Deny commercial won a Clio, Vicki received a promotion to vice-president.

A RELATIONSHIP OF EQUAL POWER

Interestingly, she also received Brian. She came to realize the role she had played in her own second-class-citizen anything-for-love undoing. Brian, it appeared, also had unfinished business. He had been the unquestioned master in both his marriage and his relationship with Vicki. The man who had had the audacity to lead an unknown woman out of a party where she was the center of attention had ultimately discovered that people can't be controlled. He had found himself successful—and alone.

He continued to pursue Vicki.

Brian was interested to find out what a relationship of equal terms might be like. Vicki's newfound awareness held the hope for him of finally experiencing a relationship of equal power. Vicki saw the opportunity to rescript an old pattern. He would stop by her office when he was in New York. They worked through the old issues over lunches. They started hammering out new ones over subsequent dinners.

Sometime after they got to breakfast, Brian moved to New York and did freelance work for six months while he looked for a suitable position.

■ ■ ■

PERSONAL POWER

Vicki had learned to express her personal power in her relationships, too. Rather than always seeking greener pastures when things got sticky, she let Brian know that her life was important and purposeful, and she was unwilling to move on a dime just to resume the relationship. Both Vicki and Brian have grown. They have discovered how to live lives where both love and work are in evidence, and are honored.

PUTTING THE PAST TO REST

I commented to Vicki that I was somewhat surprised she was getting back together with Brian.

"Well, BarBara," she replied, "it took a long time this time. No whirlwind reunion. We're both willing to grow, and that's neat. We were both in it for the wrong reasons before. Now we have a shot at a pretty good thing."

"I really give you credit, Vicki, for facing your dragons and choosing new values. It seems you both reached some self-understanding," I commented.

"Thank you, we have. I told him, 'Brian, *tous comprendre, c'est tous pardonner.'* "

"Vicki, that went over my head," I told her. "How about a translation?"

"To understand everything is to forgive everything."

Maria Stollenwerk shut herself in the darkened parlor of a previous time, her career behind a door forever closed.

Vicki Dennison eagerly faced the unlimited tomorrows unaware that her progress would be impeded by the weight of the yesterdays that accompanied her on her odyssey.

Mary Louise DeVaney had no past obligations over which the concealing draperies must be pulled. She had no baggage that would delay her trip or alter her itinerary. She knew exactly where she was going and the fastest way to get there. She just didn't know, who, then, she would be.

Mary Louise DeVaney

■

She lived many roles before finding her own.

Mary Louise DeVaney told me that she had decided very early in her life to become a Career Woman and she loved the response she got from adults when she made this announcement as a child. She told me that there was a belief in her family that anything was possible, and she loved to elaborate on this theme.

"I must have been in the third grade when I read a story about Madame Curie, I think. Then I got glasses and I felt very serious and professional, somehow. There were relatives and assorted people at our house one day when I announced, 'No powerless jobs for me. I'm going to amount to something. I'm going to be Someone Special.' And they applauded."

"THAT'S WHERE THE MONEY IS"

And special she was. She was also bright, energetic, aggressive, and possessed of a stellar analytical mind. There wasn't one reason her earlier predictions couldn't come true. She had been raised in a happy, upwardly mobile suburban household. Her parents imbued her with a strong work ethic and a deep sense of responsibility. Her engineer father led her to trust numbers, science, research, and collectively, education. Accordingly, she was an outstanding student, bright and full of curiosity. It was never a question that her family would send her to "the college of her choice," followed by the de rigueur MBA. Mary Louise—she was never called just Mary—decided to go into banking because, as she quoted Willie Sutton, "That's where the money is."

In no time at all, that's where Mary Louise was, too.

A year after her start date she married the head of marketing. He had noticed her the day she walked in wearing her dress-for-success sensible navy wool suit with the simple silk blouse and the paisley tie. With her medium-heeled navy pumps and the simple Coach shoulder bag she looked like a woman who had Learned Her Role Awareness Lessons Well. Nevertheless, the uniform of the upwardly mobile banker inadequately concealed the dynamic woman within—the woman who could hardly wait to make her mark. That's the woman who showed through the predictability of the "right clothes for a woman entering the banking profession" and that's the woman that Mark Heppler decided he couldn't live without.

THE VAULT LINE

After a series of coffee breaks that led to lunches and lunches that led to dinners, Mark led Mary Louise into the vault, telling her there was something seriously amiss and that he needed her to help correct the situation.

Mary Louise, ever the problem solver, quickly followed him

into the inner recesses. At this time his voice fell to a lower octave and took on an almost conspiratorial tone.

"Mary Louise, something here in this vault has come to my attention. It has great value—both monetary, and more important, emotional. I want you to take it and remove it in the proper manner." His voice carried great seriousness. A seriousness that was quite unusual for Mark.

She matched his tone easily. "Of course, Mark, anything to help. What can I do?"

"Take this." He thrust a small box into her hand. "Open it."

She did as she was told, and discovered a stunning diamond solitaire of rather impressive proportions. Mary Louise—who was known for not being without the proper comment or retort—could not find her voice. It had somehow deserted her. Mark was as surprised by her unprecedented silence as she was. It drove him to new levels of determination.

"I love you, Mary Louise. Marry me. Love me. Or . . . or . . . or I'll lock us in the vault. I swear I will, and we'll die in each other's arms before the time lock opens it again tomorrow morning. Either you promise to marry me or it's certain death."

Mary Louise, ever practical, found her voice and managed a small "Yes."

She kept her promise.

REALISTICALLY ASSESSED HER SITUATION

He was creative, as creative as she was practical. He was the type who would propose in a bank vault. She was the type who wore minimal jewelry: a classic watch, a single strand of pearls, and now a plain gold band albeit with that rather large diamond engagement ring. The more flexible and unpredictable and fun-loving Mark continued to be, the better Mary Louise could focus her devotion to her stance as the Total Career Woman. It seemed only what was expected of her, and consequently, what she expected of herself.

Mary Louise would subsequently explain to me that she never really considered herself to be "creative," that her talent was not for making something from nothing but reassembling what was already there. "To take somebody else's efforts—or leavings—and rearrange them into something new." Even that had proved to be difficult at the bank, where there hadn't been much room even for as undemanding a task as "rearranging."

Mary Louise felt blocked at the bank. She realistically assessed her situation there: No woman had ever been promoted beyond two levels above her, and even those were staff jobs. The bank was growing, but very slowly. There was almost no turnover among the people who stood between her and the top.

Mary Louise determined she needed to seek opportunity in a field more open to women and with a much faster pace, perhaps one she could even help to accelerate. She chose advertising.

As was the case in every other undertaking of Mary Louise's, she plunged into her homework with the dedication of the zealot. She had a new mission.

OVER FOUR HUNDRED APPLICANTS

Perkins, Scheaffer & Morrison, one of the very largest advertising agencies, was about to revitalize its moribund training program. The competition would be tough, but Mary Louise was determined to be tougher. There were over four hundred applicants for a mere ten openings in the training program, but Mary Louise had gone up against those kinds of odds before and won. She did again.

What she didn't realize, and wouldn't for some time, was that Perkins, Scheaffer & Morrison had a good shot at obtaining the McCloud Bank account. Perkins, Scheaffer & Morrison had been after that account for several years with ever-heightening activity in their pursuit of a remarkably prestigious piece of business. Mary Louise's experience at a competing bank of similar stature was very appealing to management at PS&M. Consequently, she was repeatedly questioned about her experiences during her tenure at "her" bank. It was during one of these harmless—but not too harmless—inquisitions that Mary Louise inadvertently revealed what came to be known as the "bank vault proposal," to her everlasting chagrin.

Mary Louise, of course, told it but once. That was all it took. The story was told hundreds of times after that. The version I heard, and incidentally, the first I heard of Mary Louise, included Mark standing naked in a pile of loose twenty-dollar bills and shouting, "All this can be yours." It strained credibility at the time, and I much preferred the original that was ultimately told to me by Mary Louise herself. However, anything coming out of PS&M—which had the playful industry nickname of Perverts, Sadists & Masochists—should not have stood undisputed.

THE ROLE OF AGGRESSIVE FEMALE

The training program on which Mary Louise and the other nine recent hires embarked encompassed all phases of the business, and true to form, Mary Louise found them all fascinating. However, at the program's end, only research and media had openings. Media was not something she believed would hold her interest beyond the early stages. She was afraid she could become bored. She knew her analytical skills were superb and recognized the need for more measurable arguments in advertising, so she chose the role in research.

At the time, the women's movement was gaining considerable strength. A lot of women felt they had to assume an aggressive stance to succeed. Mary Louise was no different. She became the Aggressive Female competing in a man's world. The research department had three women for every man, but the men ran it, and that's what Mary Louise wanted to do. It took her eight years, but it worked. Eight years of playing hardball and alienating co-workers and stepping on a lot of toes. But Mary Louise thought that was normal, what was expected, and the way "to play the game." It took her to senior vice-president/director of research.

Everyone was impressed.

Being head of research in a four-hundred-million-dollar agency allows not just a lot of recognition, but mammoth clout.

And many times there's a price to be paid. Somewhere about halfway up that ladder, Mary Louise surpassed Mark's salary at the bank. She was also less inclined to indulge his charming but time-consuming romantic escapades. Their marriage fell apart.

With predictable enthusiasm she threw herself into her work with a renewed interest and increased dedication.

Everyone commented on how brave she was and what a wonderful job she was doing "under the circumstances." Mary Louise simply felt less encumbered.

At a private party thrown by the management of PS&M to announce Mary Louise's appointment as director of research and the concomitant senior vice-presidency, she had a particularly interesting conversation with David Hatch, who was the director of account service at the agency, and like Mary Louise, a senior vice-president. To her surprise, he asked her to dinner the following evening so they could continue a most fascinating convergence of ideas. That appealed to her. David Hatch appealed to her: He was direct, so "no nonsense" in his approach. And that was how their affair started.

PERFORMANCE AT ALL COSTS

It was the usual trite story. He was married. But Mary Louise took great comfort in the fact that their relationship would never really go anywhere. It couldn't. She was a Career Woman, after all, and her experience had taught her that a committed relationship couldn't survive her strong-minded pursuit of power. She would never push him to leave his wife. She didn't want him to. And he clearly wouldn't do it. It was perfect: The borders were very clearly defined and they both found comfort staying within them.

In her marriage Mary Louise had been using her relationship the way many professional men use *their* home lives—for emotional release and to get "fueled up" for the next day's "performance at all costs" corporate ethos.

Mary Louise believed that *someone* had to be the nurturer, the tender of the home fires and relational values, what anthropologist Patricia McBroom describes as "the traits that cluster around feminine identity: nurturance, emotional rapport, vulnerability. . . ."

As an affair, her relationship with David was not one that needed to be *tended,* not one that needed to be consciously and conscientiously maintained. It was as much for her as it was for him, and she was comfortably powerful in it.

THE PRIME-TIME FAMILY

However verbally supportive her family had been, the old roles and rules she had seen began to speak to Mary Louise. In her internal world, the blueprint for marriage included one powerful, directed individual who brought the world home and provided for the family's *financial* and *status* needs, and one individual who maintained connection, intimacy, and spontaneity, and who provided for the family's *emotional* and *physical* needs. In this regard, she had internalized the role divisions inherent not only in her typical postwar family, but in the one next door, and the one on prime time.

Early in her career, it seemed that Mary Louise had escaped the strict role divisions of her upbringing. Actually, she had not escaped them, but traded them—*she* had sought to be the externally centered, powerful, career-directed spouse: the "husband" of her childhood. This marriage worked for a while but fell apart for many of the reasons a traditional marriage falls apart. McBroom offers this warning about the extremes of male professionalism:

> If there is anything we know from the lives of men, it is the danger of becoming lost in professional roles. The creep of professionalism constitutes a clear and present danger to intimate relationships.

Clearly, for Mary Louise, marriage could work only if she would be willing to abdicate her earlier "aggressive female" professional role and play "wife."

NO ROLES, NO RULES

But an *affair!* Because no internal script existed, she could improvise. There were no stated roles, no clear responsibilities for that type of relationship. It was a very full, happy, and productive time in her life.

David Hatch and Mary Louise DeVaney loved working together. His admiration continued to grow as her drive and independence and wonderfully analytical mind displayed itself again and again. The very fact that she made no demands on him, nor he on her (except in their professional lives at the agency), only emphasized their individual capacities for cool self-assurance.

He surprised everyone—especially Mary Louise—when he left his wife and announced he was going to marry Mary Louise. Practically the entire agency, and much of the local ad community, turned out for the wedding. Even the octogenarian Mr. Quigley came up from Palm Beach for the event. "They would have been fools not to" was the consensus. Both Mary Louise and David were very important, and their work touched everything that was done at Perkins, Scheaffer & Morrison.

It was only days later that the long-sought McCloud Bank finally awarded its business to PS&M with the added benefit of announcing they would also be responsible for rolling out the new bank card that was "destined to revolutionize the way America buys." Mary Louise would be at the forefront of this major new piece of business. So would David Hatch.

REMARKABLY OUT OF CHARACTER

Consequently, her call to me a week later came as quite a surprise. The most recent edition of a leading trade magazine featured Mary Louise on the cover and stressed her contributions to PS&M's growth, both over the long range and its most recent spurt.

We met in a garden café, a typical ladies-who-lunch spot. From what I knew of Mary Louise, the choice seemed remarkably out of character. Maybe it was simply convenient or the choice had been made without thinking. But that hardly fit the famous director of research with the keen analytical mind.

She arrived in a serious suit with a serious expression, both gray. There was not a trace of humor in her. The reason for the meeting was to ask my help in relocating her. I didn't have to break into my patented "I don't do that" speech. She knew that I didn't market people per se; that was not her intention. She also knew that she could hardly start sending out résumés at her level and that she would need my help. She wanted me to keep her in mind for any appropriate opportunities. No problem there. She said she wasn't "in any special hurry," but her manner belied the comment. Her explanation for all of this: "I just feel the need for a change." I questioned her on this, but she insisted she just wanted a change and would not elaborate.

I didn't buy it for a minute. I did not yet understand her motivation and this sudden shift in priorities. Just the same, at this point I was willing to represent her, and "keeping her in mind" was a snap.

A POTENTIAL FOR POWER

Several weeks later I called her regarding an exciting line opening in the manufacturing sector at an innovative electronics company with astonishing visibility. Here was an opportunity to be part of something tangible that would find its way into millions of homes and lives.

But not Mary Louise's life. She had all kinds of reasons why this would not be right for her, none of which held up from a career or personal standpoint. In fact, it was a huge step upward in her career and a chance to play on an international stage, but she simply "didn't feel this would be the thing to do at this moment."

(As a side note, the man who took the job for which I wanted to present Mary Louise is now the CEO of that company. He has made so much money through the company's generous stock option plan that he could quit working today and live very well. But he won't quit, certainly not for a long time. He's simply having too much fun. Every year, on his anniversary date, the board has managed to find something wonderful to do for him. He has never failed to send me three dozen yellow roses on the same date.)

A few months later I tried to reach Mary Louise again with an opportunity I believed would be perfect for her—and she it. I was told she had left PS&M the week before to take a staff job with an insurance company.

For the life of me, I couldn't fathom why.

TAKE MY WIFE, PLEASE

A couple of years later I had the occasion to talk with a great guy who was a managing partner with Perkins, Scheaffer & Morrison. I wanted to tell him about an assignment I had from a new client in Atlanta who wanted a major talent who could come in and reshape his Atlanta agency. It was an equity position. The candidate—David Hatch—jumped at it.

"Will this present a problem for your wife, David?" I asked carefully. I didn't know if Mary Louise would have mentioned to him that I had known her for years.

"She won't care," he responded. "One job is the same as the next to her." It was said with bitterness and not a trace of humor.

Listening to him, I reflected that although I had known Mary Louise for years, I must not really have known her at all. Or perhaps she had not known herself.

"So you know that your wife's career will not be a deterrent to relocation?"

"BarBara, you know my wife. She used to be Mary Louise DeVaney."

Used to be! What an idea.

. . .

THE ROLE OF SUBMISSIVE FEMALE

As things unfolded and I grew to know David Hatch much better during the interviewing process, he revealed that Mary Louise was determined not to make the same mistakes in their marriage that she felt she had made when she was married to her first husband. She refused to "compete in the market-place." So she assumed, what to her, was the proper "role" of the good wife, the second-class citizen. Despite David's many arguments against this, he could not get through to Mary Louise.

The real tragedy, as great as the waste of her talents, was that David—like Amanda's husband, Ted Spencer—didn't want that kind of subordinate. David wanted a partner. That's why he had fallen in love with Mary Louise. That's why he left his wife to marry her.

David accepted the position in Atlanta. The agency now bears his name as well as those of the founders. He has gradually replaced them through a dramatic leveraged buyout that left him, and his new partners, in control of a very dynamic agency. He's having a wonderful time doing exactly what he knows he does best. But he's doing it without Mary Louise—not only in the agency, but in his life as well.

The marriage ended soon after they moved to Atlanta.

"WHO ARE YOU? WHAT DO YOU WANT?"

I've seen her many times since, for a while in Boston, where she relocated after Atlanta, and finally in New York, where she is today. We usually meet for lunch. And I always ask the same questions: "Who are you? What do you want?"

She has finally accepted the concept that there is a lifescript that many of us have to fight very hard to break away from.

That we must pioneer our own lives and recast our lifescripts or forevermore be shackled to them. The failure of both of her marriages and the resulting crises forced her to discover that she wants to express her ideas in the business world and, more important, can enjoy intimate relationships without having to serve them.

She's off to a good start.

THE PENDULUM SWINGS

Anthropologist Patricia McBroom illuminates a theory of identity that describes the process of becoming oneself through adapting to various roles, various societal expectations:

> Once having dressed and acted the part, once having been recognized and accepted in the new role, people sooner or later regain their individuality . . . the self has several hats and several identities, which draw on and express different talents, desires and strengths. A key thing to know about this theory of identity is that the I, the central decision maker and motivator of life, stands above, and encompasses both feminine and professional identities. Although people may be caught in their roles from time to time and allow themselves to be defined by their jobs, (whether in finance or motherhood) . . . [they] struggle to master their jobs. They want to control their lives rather than be imprisoned by a script in the social order.

Mary Louise DeVaney was one who struggled with roles for two decades. She had internalized a family and societal script that allowed only for corporate or personal involvement, never both. Men rarely have this internal split. The traits of masculine personality that are prized in the workplace usually match those that are expected of men in the home environment as well.

In order for Mary Louise to achieve integration between femininity and adulthood, she first had to try on both "hats," and wear each role fully. Because her parents' gender divisions was so total, seeking a balance first required a violent pendulum swing between the two options.

Ultimately, Mary Louise had experienced enough of both roles in her own adult life to be able to integrate them and find a cohesive sense of self. In my parlance, she became a woman who owns her own power.

Which, in my view, is a prerequisite for corporate power.

Mary Louise's pendulum swings cost her time. A lot of time. She believes that although she worked, and very hard at times, she had no career direction or focus for at least seven years. She had to play "catch-up" for a year to reacclimate herself. She also believes her one-or-the-other role-playing was a factor in her not having children.

"My mother not only had children, she lived in the world of children and school and good nutrition and piano lessons. When I married David I thought we might have kids, but our marriage seemed off-balance pretty much from the start.

"And then I thought, 'I'll be home with them all the time! I'll *become* my mother!' and I had worked so hard specifically *not* to do that! I felt terribly stuck, like I couldn't decide, truly, to *do* anything."

"How long was this true?" I asked her.

"Oh, the whole time David and I were married, I guess. We were such good friends before, but then"—she laughed ironically—"but then, we became husband and wife."

■   ■   ■

THE CLOCK TICKS

Mary Louise paused, and a sad expression crossed her face. A look of acceptance quickly replaced it.

"I've thought about it, BarBara—I could have children now. I could be director of research, or CEO, or whatever, and still have children."

"But wasn't that always true? What's the difference now?" I asked.

"Five years ago, having children would have meant I'd be a *mother.* Now I could be an executive VP who just happened to have kids."

"Sounds terrific."

"Yeah, but I'm forty-four."

We smiled at each other. Smiles that attested to our mutual recognition of the reality of time and choices made. Mary Louise's smile turned into a full-fledged grin. "Not too old to be a CEO," she said.

"Not by a long shot," I agreed.

She's back in advertising as director of research at a medium-size agency and has done some innovative things that are beginning to be noticed by a field eager to anoint success. She's also dating a professor at Columbia. He has two teenage sons.

"Tell me about them," I asked.

"The professor? Or the kids?"

"All of the above, I've got the time," I replied.

"You know, BarBara, so do I. The kids are getting used to me. They asked me when I was going to become their 'wicked stepmother.' I told them they'd be the second and third to know. Their father is eager to be first." She broke into a wide, wonderful smile. "He finds me stimulating." She paused before continuing, and then stressed, "Fascinating."

She *was* stimulating. She *was* fascinating. And just maybe she was comfortable with those good things for the first time and didn't see them as threatening, but quite simply there.

At our last lunch together we joked about all the time we had known each other, and yet, I had never placed Mary Louise in a position. I convinced her that hardly mattered: I had learned so much from her. She laughed and said, "Ironically, so have I."

She no longer looked and dressed like the warden at a women's prison. She was in a soft silk print. I saw the woman she was, who had been hidden in all those other roles. And she was smiling.

Unlike any of the various Mary Louise DeVaneys of the previous twenty years, the one before me was, at last, a fully integrated adult who finally owned her own power. If she could catch up quickly enough to compete with the men who had *not* lost several years of career building, she could make a great CEO.

Maria Stollenwerk was hobbled by a patriarchy of the most intimate nature, her father's.

Vicki Dennison, who would have laughed at such obvious shackles, was still controlled by a large, encompassing, systemic patriarchy—the Army—a faceless father with stringent rules and unquestioned needs.

Mary Louise DeVaney had a great father and a terrific mother and the freedom to adapt, which she did—repeatedly—like a chameleon.

Catherine Ames had none of those problems. She had the potential and promise of unprecedented power because she never hesitated to break the rules. Except one. The one she didn't recognize.

CATHERINE AMES

∎

She had a large vision, but couldn't see herself in it.

CHICAGO WAS in hibernation, refusing to budge until there was a guarantee of spring. The seasonal lull and accompanying lethargy had set in. The twinkle lights had already been removed from the trees lining Michigan Avenue, and all that was left was a moody aftermath and ankle-deep slush.

Unlike the movies, there is no background music in life to suggest an impending event or indicate the prevailing mood. If there were, that morning might have been filled with piercing violins with nervous staccato outbursts, or an eerie Moog synthesizer with its electronic red flags.

As it was, the whole team at Bools was having a wonderful time that early day in January. The mood was celebratory. I had just received a call from London from a client for whom I had just completed an executive search for the head of their pan-European division. Then Susan came into the conference room and said, "BarBara, it's Jim Culpepper."

· · ·

AN OUTPLACEMENT

Jim and I didn't have the chance to talk to each other very often. When we did, it was never small talk.

I had first met Jim many years earlier, when he had been president of his company, Lincoln Foods, Inc. He had called me to discuss a project that led to a five-year consulting job with him. He was then in line to become CEO and to run the company. In the years prior to that event, he had wanted to put himself in a readiness position based on his overall business plan. I designed a people plan covering the issues of evaluation, development, recruitment, and deployment to complement his vision for the business. In the course of this work, he engaged me in matters concerning his present and future role in the company and in the marketplace.

Now Jim was the CEO of LCI, located in Louisville, with offices and factories around the world. Jim (in an industry coup) had earlier spearheaded the acquisition of Continental Foods, Inc. Since it wouldn't do to have Lincoln Continental Foods—it would sound too much like you'd be eating hubcaps—it became LCI. Although insiders would call it Lincoln Foods for years to come, LCI was officially launched with appropriate fanfare and the requisite redesign of their corporate logo. The new LCI name quickly appeared on all sorts of cans and boxes; potato chips, a line of bicycles (where the Lincoln Continental name may have been a plus), and their famous line of dairy products which included a gourmet ice cream manufactured in a suburban factory but bearing a Scandinavian name. Jim was a direct, no-nonsense person, and a long-standing client with whom I enjoyed working. In view of recent events, however, I picked up the phone with a certain trepidation.

"Hi, Jim. What can I do for you?"

"You don't usually do outplacements, do you, BarBara?"

He sounded tired. There was no musical accompaniment, but I knew what was coming.

"Not usually," I answered carefully. I thought of my long association with Jim and LCI. "But I have done a few," and then, as an afterthought, "in special cases."

"This *is* a special case."

"Catherine," I said simply.

"Catherine," he confirmed with a heavy sigh.

We discussed the particulars for over half an hour. Jim had thought things through very carefully. He had a luncheon appointment with Catherine that very day and would tell her then, away from the office. Because I had agreed to handle the outplacement, he would tell her that Bools & Associates was under contract by LCI to advise and aid her in relocating. There would be an extremely generous severance package. The official story could be whatever Catherine wanted. If she preferred to announce her resignation, Jim would not interfere, although he would certainly advise against it. The board of directors already knew the truth. The head of personnel soon would. Given her level, a number of people would have to be involved in the legalization of a termination. Jim knew that big, juicy secrets like this never remained secrets for long. He finally said to me, "BarBara, we must convince Catherine that facing up to a firing garners more respect than faking a resignation." He paused. "I'll be in touch." With that he hung up.

News travels fast in any small community. And the community of marketing and advertising is both small and visible, with a highly developed grapevine, both formal and informal. Certainly, Jim and I were agreed—Catherine would be better off in the long run admitting the truth of her firing. Truth is always the best policy.

Before I could return to the group in the conference room, Susan buzzed to say that Jim Culpepper was back on the phone.

As always, he started right out talking. "There is one bright spot, BarBara."

"I can't imagine what that might be," I answered.

"Of course you also have the search assignment for her replacement." He added, "We haven't got a lot of time," and abruptly hung up.

A CAREER IN CRISIS

Actually, I would have preferred that neither assignment was necessary. Our company had a long history of bringing the best and the brightest to LCI, Catherine being one of them. Her contribution to LCI had been extraordinary. I knew Catherine well, and wanted very much to help her get back on track. I was in a unique position to best handle both assignments, and I always enjoyed working with LCI.

Better still would have been Catherine's continued career success and well-being. But her career was in crisis. I needed to sort out what had gone wrong.

Catherine Ames had always been bright and capable, but she was more than that. She was a visionary. Part of the excitement for me of specializing my practice in marketing and advertising is that what happens here generally affects the rest of our society. I was glad that Catherine Ames was in such a visible, trend-setting arena. I looked forward to living in a society influenced by her visions and contributions.

A POWERHOUSE EXECUTIVE

My mind drifted to the first time I saw Catherine Ames. She was going to be in Chicago for a conference, and I had arranged lunch to meet this marketing dynamo with whom I'd spoken on occasion. I had followed Catherine's rapid career rise for three years, with ever-mixed emotions of excitement and caution. As I awaited her at the restaurant, I wondered, "Is this the woman who will finally go the distance, or is she this year's installment of fast-track women who derail?"

Then Catherine arrived. She was a stunner. Tall, slim, even regal, with hair the color of midnight, pulled straight back into a bun. Nothing about her seemed studied. And certainly nothing was superfluous. She wore a watch and a wedding ring and no other jewelry. Black wool slacks. A matching turtleneck. The classic Burberry trench coat. Her eyes shone with intelligence and purpose. She was cool and controlled and she drew the attention of the room. Had Hitchcock fancied brunettes rather than blondes, Catherine would have been his icon.

She lived up to her advance reputation. I was fascinated with her. Here finally was a powerhouse female executive with a hunger for advancement and a desire to impact her business. She was polished, brilliant, and a clear, unique thinker. The dynamic advancements she had brought to her company were myriad and far-reaching. She had become a cornerstone executive of an exciting new regime at her agency, and the whole industry was paying close attention. The woman was a star.

Over the next year or so we had lunch on several occasions. We always talked about the business we had chosen to be in. We talked about marketing, about the changing consumer, about global advertising trends. We were both fundamentally turned on by our work and found great joy in discussing it with each other. We talked about how much impact one individual can have on the industry. Catherine passionately believed in the power of a single individual.

She once told me, "BarBara, if you have the right ideas—*solutions* in this world—and you know they're right, then you need as much authority and support as possible so that you can make them real. Appropriate solutions should never be lost." Her eyes shone.

Catherine saw an opportunity through her work to impact positively on world nutrition and food supply. She contributed her time and expertise to many organizations that gave her access to foreign market leaders. I greatly admire people who are conscious of their own power. The possibilities for positive change through the exercise of that power are stimulating.

We shared our visions. These lunches always seemed to end too quickly. I loved the exchange of ideas and barely noticed that in a year Catherine had never mentioned anything of her personal life.

"YOU'D LIKE MY HUSBAND"

At one lunch, however, something off-center started to emerge. Catherine suddenly began talking about her family. In and of itself, this wouldn't have been unusual. Over time, many business associates share glimpses of their personal lives. In fact, I always ask about family histories, wanting a fuller picture, because experience has proven that an individual's past is the best indicator of future results. Catherine, however, had consistently maintained a professional focus, talking only about work. I had chalked this up to her strong career commitment, and a likely reason for her remarkable success. So, although it was uncharacteristic of Catherine to be personally revealing, it wasn't the topic of her family that struck me as odd, but her radical change of manner and demeanor.

The facts spilled out in a tumble to be sorted later. Not at all Catherine's usual organized, precise, controlled delivery. Catherine started speaking of her daughter, Emma, and seemed to transform into a budding teenager herself. Her inflection and gestures shifted from her typical moderation to a broader, less graceful mode. She gushed and giggled as she told me about her daughter: She had not yet settled on boys per se but was enraptured with Hayden and Handel and, in an off moment, Springsteen. She wanted to be an opera singer or a sculptor or a lawyer or a nun or some combination of the above. We were laughing at the possible combinations. A singing nun had been done, but combine nun and judge and it would simplify one's wardrobe.

In talking about Emma, Catherine briefly mentioned the twins and their older brother, Sam. I inquired further, and Catherine's laughter stopped.

"Sam. Sam has been missing for three months. Where he is, how he is, I don't know." Something about her toneless delivery prevented me from asking anything further. She was not about to say more.

There was just a moment's silence and then Catherine spoke again. "You'd like my husband." She became quite animated talking about him. She described him as strong, talented, the rock of the family. But when I asked more about him, her answers grew vague. I gathered he owned his own business and was some type of consultant and that he carefully tailored his services to the needs of each client. He conducted seminars, but when I inquired for more information about them— and him—Catherine changed the subject and returned to our more habitual conversational arena—business. She proceeded to outline a particular marketing concept she was about to introduce.

AN UNPRECEDENTED PERK

At the time, I wondered about the changes in direction our lunch discussion had taken. I believed it had something to do with having a missing son. But it was not until some months later that the peculiarities Catherine had shown took on added significance. A management supervisor from Catherine's agency called and asked if I might meet with him the next time I was in New York. He wanted to talk to me about his career.

I had an opportunity to meet with him just two weeks later. We met for lunch at my hotel. I arrived downstairs on time, and he was already there, finishing a drink. It didn't take long for me to discover that he was very bitter about recent developments at the agency. He had worked in conjunction with Catherine. But there was a new guard forming in top management, with new rules, and a distinctly different culture. Because she was bright and capable and picking up clients right and left, Catherine was a key player. This man clearly had been left behind in the scramble. He had been discredited and disenfranchised. Dismissal might be next. Or worse, he might float in that kind of limbo where you have no accounts and no responsibility and you might as well be wearing a sign that says "leper." He was confused and angry.

As he continued to complain, I sensed a poetic justice. Here was a man famous for "cutting 'em off at the knees." He understood the game, and had played it to his advantage for years. Now politically wounded himself, he was crying as loudly as any of his victims ever had. But he seemed resilient—and anger would serve him better at this juncture than would shock or depression. Listening to him, he already had plans for his future. He would soon recoup. Then he said something about Catherine that really caught my attention.

"Well, her track record's amazing. That's for sure. I'll be damned if I can figure out why they put up with her family bullshit." He quieted for just a moment and then said in a deadpan tone, "Can you imagine if I had asked for an office for my wife?"

"I don't get it. What do you mean, 'office for your wife'?"

"They like to keep it quiet. Oh, God, do they like to keep it quiet." He leaned forward and dropped his voice. "Two years ago Catherine Ames asked for an office for her husband so he could start a business or something. Who knows what he does with it. The whole thing's insane, if you ask me." Of course, I didn't have to ask him; he was off and running now. "Catherine not only wanted an office for him but she fucking insisted that he have access to all office support facilities: copiers, typewriters, Federal Express pickups, secretarial help, his own phone. And of course—this is my personal favorite"—he straightened, crossed his ankles, and did a passable imitation of Catherine—" 'it would be humiliating for Warren to occupy an office smaller than mine.' "

I was shocked by this bit of news, or gossip, and started checking around. The bizarre tale was true. Catherine's agency occupied five floors of some of the most expensive office space in Manhattan; and on one of those floors was a very desirable office whose occupant didn't even work for the agency. But his wife did.

POWER SYMBOLS

Obviously, it was important to Catherine that her husband be granted all the trappings of a man achieving success and consequence. "Be granted" not "earn." In fact, Catherine pushed beyond all convention with this request. Her substantial work performance made her credit-worthy, obviously, but it struck me as highly questionable judgment on her part to call in her chips in this way. Surely the Ameses could afford to rent acceptable office space elsewhere. I felt genuine confusion as I tried to determine what possible priorities and motives would lead Catherine to secure such power symbols for her husband at the risk of her own credibility.

A STAR'S REQUESTS

A week later, business again took me to Manhattan, where Catherine worked, and I had been asked to lunch by one of the managing partners of her agency. We were discussing the new direction of the agency, and Catherine was naturally a prime topic of our conversation. Our discussion also included the rapidly changing perception of the agency within the industry. The time was perfect to discuss the growing street knowledge of Catherine's husband's strange office arrangement. While my impulse was to blurt out my amazement, I opted for a more subdued approach and asked, instead, if this was a new type of employee perk.

He answered, rather sheepishly, "No, BarBara, these requests were totally without precedent and we all thought they were totally inappropriate. Heaven forbid anyone else would ask for similar arrangements."

Puzzled, I asked, "Then *why* did you do it?"

He laughed at my question. A somewhat weary laugh. Then he said, "BarBara, we're all part of show business. Catherine's a star. And a star's requests are never too outrageous."

AN EXPLOITATION OF POWER?

It was clear that Catherine's performance and value warranted the granting of such an unusual perquisite. I had become aware, over the years, of many unusual perks. One company relocated a man whose children had been in excellent public schools in California, so they paid for private schooling for all four of his children. Another boarded a horse for a new vice-president. A third provided a personal shopper and an account at Brooks Brothers for a streetwise but unfashionable executive they deemed needed sprucing up. Unusual perks hardly surprised me. But they usually shared a common trait that was absent from this oddity of Catherine's: out-of-the-ordinary perquisites are kept private, undisclosed. The less known and noticeable, the better. An office for Catherine's husband was so very blatant that it begged accusations that this was an exploitation of power. I wondered at Catherine's judgment. I wondered as well what kind of person Catherine's husband could be.

"AT HER HUSBAND'S SIDE"

A few weeks later I finally met him at an industry awards dinner. I discovered that Warren Ames rather fit Catherine's description of him. He was quite tall and ruggedly handsome with a confident, take-charge manner and an incredible voice. He was everything Catherine had said he would be. And one more that she hadn't mentioned: he was flashy. As flashy and flamboyant as I had known her to be serene and understated.

I was quite taken aback by Warren at the start. No sooner had Catherine introduced us than he launched into a boisterous monologue about world events. He allowed no "hello," no social warm-up, and certainly no discussion. I noted that he didn't connect at all; he made pronouncements. He would be as difficult to get to know as he was to ignore.

And Catherine! The difference in her presentation was astonishing. The woman before me could be described only as "at her husband's side," if anyone would care to describe her at all. Her eyes—which had always contained intelligence and purpose—were turned toward her husband with deference and awe. Her usually swept-back hair hung to her waist in a style that struck me as adolescent. She expressed no opinions, speaking only to accentuate a point of Warren's or divert someone else's interjection. Occasionally, she seemed giddy, even flirtatious. Silently, I was relieved that Catherine was not on that evening's speaker's platform.

During the ensuing months, facts about Catherine's husband started to emerge. It was widely growing knowledge that he'd start a business (from *his* office at *her* agency) and then fold it a few months later only to start a new one. He'd been to grad school in journalism but hadn't completed his thesis. He had claimed to be a publishing agent for a year but had never produced an author or a publisher. All his business efforts were vague and unspecific and eventually faded away. The facts kept adding up that—professionally, at least—he didn't add up to much of anything. But Catherine clearly thought he was wonderful.

AN OPPORTUNITY WITHOUT A CEILING

Despite my concern about Catherine's perspective regarding her husband, she had consistently shown herself to be perceptive and on-target about her career. The far-reaching changes at her agency had strengthened her position and she had more than risen to the occasion. She was indeed a star.

Consequently, when a major opportunity came along that would dramatically enhance Catherine's career, I could hardly wait to present it to her. For three years Catherine had talked about her visions, her desire to influence and contribute. Although Bools & Associates had worked on many assignments calling for backgrounds similar to Catherine's, this was the first opportunity that would truly expand her power, her reach. That Catherine wanted to exercise her visions was clear. This new position would provide her a broader arena. Perhaps even more exciting, this was an opportunity without a ceiling.

When I called, Catherine told me my timing was perfect. She recently had been talking with a giant real estate investment conglomerate in the Sunbelt about a key position to spearhead all marketing and advertising for their many divisions. Although it would have been a forward move for her in many ways, the position lacked what she had grown to desire: involvement with packaged-goods marketing on a global scale and communication with the consumer through the rapidly changing channels of the media.

The position I presented gave her both the power and the marketing arena: director of marketing for Lincoln Foods.

Catherine was now part of a comprehensive search I had just begun. Management had specifically requested that qualified women be included, and presented to the board of directors during the final selection process.

I felt it a matter of course to address the now infamous office provided for Warren. I asked Catherine directly to comment on that unusual arrangement.

With a very lighthearted tone, she insisted: "Granted it was without precedent, but the circumstances surrounding it *were* extraordinary. The agency was looking for ways to reward me. I was helping Warren market his new company at a very crucial moment in its development. The agency was also provided a highly unusual opportunity to display the lengths it would go to to ensure optimum working conditions for one of its management team. It was a one-time, win-win situation." And then in a surprisingly conspiratorial tone: "You know how advertising agencies are, BarBara, people fly to Paris for lunch."

"No one I know. Most of the good ones are too busy and skip lunch altogether."

"BarBara, it was an isolated incident." And then with pronounced emphasis: "It won't need to happen again."

I bought that.

A CARICATURE OF THE EXECUTIVE
WOMAN

In the second stage of the search, Bools & Associates presented six semi-finalists to Lincoln Foods' management. In addition to Catherine, there had been only one other woman. Her credentials were outstanding. She had consistently found new solutions that produced winning results, but the consensus of the management team was that her personality was too rigid. She seemed almost a caricature of the Executive Woman, right down to her sensible shoes. One had the feeling her Nikes were under a chair in the lobby. She seemed absorbed in the role rather than in the work itself (much like Mary Louise DeVaney in the first half of her career). One of the management team ventured that her outfit and firm handshake and too new briefcase were that of a recent MBA, not a confident, independent, experienced risk-taker. She had come from a male-dominated corporate culture and was behaving accordingly. She had misread the clues that indicated Lincoln Foods' values encouraged independent styles as well as independent work. Though impressed by her track record, she was scratched. My Search Status Report would read: "Client's remarks: Predictable, no independent style." Qualifications aside, it was difficult to see through the cliché.

PRACTICED IN THE GAME

The other four were all men, around the forty-year-old mark. This would have been, in all probability, the last career move the victor would be making and the sense of that was palpable. As animals can smell fear, I have learned to smell ambition, and its close cousin, competition.

These four were all professional, practiced in the game. Each had presented himself, in one form or another, a hundred times before and knew the routine and how to get through it. How much weight to give to his unique abilities as well as his ability to be a team player. How much flexibility. How much firmness. Each knew when to use military or sports metaphors and how—and when—to slip in the suitable reference to Yale or Princeton or Culpepper's alma mater. When to be light and humorous. When to be no-nonsense. When to turn on the charm. When to let that firm jaw say everything. Each worked the room like a master.

One of these four emerged from the pack. It was to be he and Catherine who would be presenting to the board of directors. Even though I have learned to fight my hunches in this business—I'd rather be a professional than a gambler—I knew instinctively that Lincoln Foods' next director of marketing would be Catherine Ames.

A WOMAN OF SUBSTANCE

Of all the candidates throughout this search, Catherine had prepared the most comprehensive, on-target presentation of herself. She had prepared a twenty-page dossier including case studies, family history, and a charming and provocative piece on her personal philosophy of life and work in combination. She had related everything to the needs and goals of Lincoln Foods. All this, and she kept her résumé to one clean, clear, concise page of straightforward career history. (I mention this because a résumé tells so much about a person's ego and sense of self-worth. She was confident enough to give only the bare minimum of facts, letting them speak for themselves.) When it came to the work, she was generous of spirit and lavish with her praise for others' efforts and successes. Her insights into Lincoln Foods, their problems, and their opportunities captured every man in the room. Catherine's substance was clear.

After she completed her presentation and left, there was just the briefest of polite logistical discussion regarding the other candidates, with intelligent but unimpassioned emphasis on the male finalist. Following those requisite amenities, the conversation turned to Catherine. There was an electricity in the room as everyone discussed the direction of Lincoln Foods and the role of marketing as Catherine would play it.

Of course, Jim Culpepper, as CEO, had more to say and

contribute than any of the others on the management team—maybe *all* of the others—but his preferred modus operandi was to hang back and withhold his input until the very last minute. Years before, I hadn't fully understood this about him, and had felt occasionally frustrated when he appeared unable to make a decision, seeming to vacillate. Experience taught me instead that Jim was very decisive but determined to hear everyone's honest opinion, unbiased by his own, as he knew would happen if he allowed his attitude to surface too early in the process. Especially with this position, Jim wanted to assess a potential candidate's "fit" with his other key managers.

After hearing the group's discussion, Jim did something a little out of character—but hardly at great risk—and announced, "I think we all know who our next director of marketing must be." No one took exception.

I left shortly thereafter, as the regular board meeting was about to commence. On my way out, Jim took me aside to say: "BarBara, you've done a great job. We want Catherine. We intend to get her, whatever it takes. Bring her on board."

A WIN-WIN SITUATION

This was the final lap of a search—the part I enjoyed the most. In two days of phone calls with Jim and Catherine, I had ironed out the particulars. Her salary would be increased twenty percent from her present job. She would receive a generous sign-on bonus. Jim wanted the guarantee of a three-year contract. I knew Catherine to be a risk-taker, and was concerned that she might not want to agree to such a long-term commitment. Actually, she felt this to be a strong match for her, and had no problem whatsoever. However, she did insist on their agreement to provide whatever resources would be needed to accomplish what she deemed necessary.

Lincoln agreed. The negotiations were over. It was one of the cleanest closings I had ever handled—both Jim and Catherine were eminently fair in their requests. They shared the same goal: the growth of Lincoln Foods. All parties were happy. Even the lawyers relaxed once they discovered no one had to assume an adversarial role—a true win-win situation.

Catherine relocated her family with her usual no-nonsense efficiency. In one week she and Warren had sold their Manhattan town house and found a beautiful sprawling almost-mansion near Louisville, which had been owned by a Xerox executive who had transferred to the East Coast a month earlier. Warren had attended college with the wife of the Xerox executive, and had smoothed the way for a quick sale. The couple also helped get the Ames children into an exclusive private school in the area. Sam was still missing. Catherine and her family were quickly and comfortably settled.

Then Catherine took a week off and went to an island before starting her new career. She insisted she was taking only her bathing suit, plenty of suntan lotion, and a seven-hundred-page beach book. What she didn't mention was that she also packed a portable computer and a suitcase full of data on Lincoln Foods. And, interestingly, on Continental Foods as well. When she began her job two weeks later, she had not only won the race, she wasn't even breathing hard.

And she did very well.

A RESOURCE FOR CATHERINE

A few months into her job at Lincoln, she asked for, and got, an office for Warren. After all, she reasoned, had they not agreed that Catherine would be provided the resources to facilitate her position? Warren was a resource for Catherine; a nice, big, cushy office was a resource for Warren. Surprised,

Jim and Lincoln Foods nonetheless provided the office and accouterments without hesitation.

Later that year Catherine's son was found dead from a drug overdose. Warren suffered a "nervous breakdown." Catherine missed three days' work. Jim Culpepper offered her an extended leave of absence on full salary. She thanked him and kept right on working.

(As shocking and off-balance as this may seem, others with similar tragedies have reacted the same way. Over the years I have worked with several men who lost children to illness, suicide, or accidents. To a man, they all expressed how grateful they were for their work, how jumping right back in had helped them through their crisis.)

PROFITS ROSE SIGNIFICANTLY

During this time, profits rose significantly. Jim Culpepper pulled off the acquisition of Continental Foods that would make him a corporate legend. Catherine was promoted to executive vice-president/international director of marketing with all of the Lincoln—now LCI—foreign subsidiaries reporting to her. This, of course, was on top of her ongoing responsibilities.

In the three years since Jim Culpepper hired Catherine Ames, she had built four divisions and unified the message of her company throughout the world. She also had played a major role in the remarkably friendly takeover of Continental Foods and the subtle blending of their two corporate cultures into a single and very dynamic entity now called LCI. Internal functions and divisions were strengthened through Catherine's unflagging efforts. The image of the new company with the consumer and the stockholder went straight up. So did the stock.

Jim was so ecstatic about Catherine's contributions that

Bools & Associates was put on retainer with LCI and awarded the lion's share of their most significant executive search assignments.

"READY FOR THE PRESIDENCY"

Lunches with Catherine continued, usually when we were both in New York, but also at the LCI cafeteria when I was visiting Louisville, and once when we were both in Dallas. One day Catherine and I met and talked about all the improvements she had made and the dynamics of her most recent plans. Her enthusiasm was so contagious I couldn't help but revel in it. I admired the brightness of her future and wanted to let her know it. "You know, Catherine, any day now you're going to be ready for the presidency."

She straightened ever so slightly in her chair, actually repositioned herself (more than I realized at the time), looked at me directly, and said, "Oh, no, BarBara, it won't have to come to that."

Recalling that moment gives me chills to this day. I didn't understand what she meant at all, but I knew her words made me uncomfortable and oddly ill at ease. I asked her to elaborate.

A HIDDEN MOTIVATION

She was only too happy to expound upon what was, to her, eminently obvious. "One of these days, BarBara, and it will be soon now, Warren's business is going to take off and I'll be there to help him with the marketing of it. In the meantime, my career growth teaches me more about marketing and provides him proper lead time and capitalization."

I was shocked. Her long-term goal might be her own success, but her longest-term goal was *his* success.

She downplayed her own true power, speaking of her work as merely a learning experience due to financial necessity. But while the needs Catherine cited were circumstantial, I suspected the arrangement the couple had was determined less by convenience than by mutual self-defeating needs. Their unspoken "arrangement" seemed to be two-pronged: In reality, she expressed high and he low competency, while in fantasy, the situation was one of subordinate wife/successful husband. Catherine's orientation was clearly relational, and the reality of her situation was clearly below her conscious awareness.

Catherine had always taken outrageous risks for Warren. But now I gleaned a hidden motivation: that she took those risks for Warren's well-being, for his future, because "someday" *he* would provide for *her*. Her innovation, vision, spirit, her breathtaking talents were being exercised only until such time as her husband would shine. I was stunned at the realization: Catherine was only playing at working.

THE MARIONETTE

Relationships based on significant inequality are not healthy, and exact a tremendous toll on both partners. The greatest cost is that individual power and expression must be foregone, subjugated to the cyclical dynamic of the relationship. In a tightly woven interdependency, it can be difficult to determine who is actually the marionette and who is pulling the strings. Capable, intelligent, respected, and very highly paid Catherine Ames would, at first glance, *seem* to be stronger than her blustery ne'er-do-well husband. But consider Dr. Susan Forward's account of a certain type of controlling misogynist, the "tragic hero":

> [He] sees himself as an innocent victim of other
> people's chicanery and . . . has an extensive history
> of unemployment and financial chaos; he often has
> to be supported by his partner.
>
> Unable to recognize how he orchestrates his own
> disasters, he sees the woman who is supporting him
> as the enemy.

In *Men Who Hate Women and the Women Who Love Them,*
Forward's sub-chapter, "The Paradox of the Powerful
Woman," describes women who are "emotionally dependent
on their misogynistic partners" but are "extremely independent in other areas of their lives." She relates the story of one
woman who ran two businesses, and was the sole support of
her husband and three children from two marriages. Of this
type of "powerful woman," Forward says:

> Her sense of self-worth is tied to his assessment of
> her, no matter what other accomplishments she has
> achieved in her life.
>
> Her need for her partner's love is the most important thing in her life. The prizes of success, financial gain, status, and prestige pale in comparison
> to that need.

Thus, despite the actual *situation* of who is more competent
and accomplished in the world, no matter who supports the
family, a certain type of woman's deep-seated need for *relationship* can cause her to be emotionally controlled by a man.
Thus, her entire career is experienced within the context of
her subservience to another.

Psychiatrist Jean Baker Miller makes a similar statement:

> People liable to depression are often very active,
> very forceful; it is organized around a single pursuit—seeking affiliation in the only form that seems

possible: "I will do anything if only you will let me
stay in this kind of relationship to you."

The realization that Catherine was looking upon her role as
merely provisional deeply concerned me. Catherine was unable to evaluate the faults of Warren's character so obvious to
everyone else. Rather than recognizing her husband for whom
he really was, she saw only what he could be, or what his role
called for.

An additional insight found its way to my consciousness.
Catherine found great satisfaction in her work—I had no
doubt of that. Therefore, if her internal fantasy called for her
to abdicate her career upon Warren's success, wouldn't she,
subconsciously, have a tremendous stake in his remaining dependent and floundering?

MOTIVATED BY TRAGEDY

However, her career was more than safe for the time being,
because her husband's was in shambles. Their son's death had
shaken Warren's world significantly. As part of his recovery,
and perhaps motivated by the tragedy, he pursued a new
personal calling. He closed down his business—what was left
of it—and decided to join the campaign against drugs. The
crisis was the impetus for him to seek involvement in crusade,
thus giving purpose and meaning to his life.

Warren traveled extensively, and during the first two years
of his absence, the family met sporadically on weekends in
different cities. Catherine seemed more energetic and ambitious than ever during this period. She had gone beyond revi-
talizing her departments and was having an effect on the
industry as well. Personally, I found her wittier and even
brighter than she had always been, as well as more relaxed and
confident, which I wouldn't have thought possible.

Crises, whether brought about by positive or negative events, even an event as terrible as the loss of a child, many times become the catalyst for change and growth. While the significance of Warren's new self-focus was not yet clear, their living arrangements portended a change in their complicit, emotionally parasitic marriage. Sam's death, Warren's lengthy absence, and his possible steps toward a healthier adult identity hadn't seemed to hurt Catherine one bit.

RAISON D'ÊTRE

At Christmastime she broke free two days early and flew to join Warren, arranging for the children to follow early the next week. She was back within a day. Warren had announced he was leaving her and filing for divorce. Shortly thereafter, Catherine was hospitalized for nearly three months because of severe depression.

What had been important to Catherine was not so much her husband's presence as the continuation of their mutual dependency, which served to sustain her in her various roles.

To many people in the industry, Warren had appeared little more than a financial drain and embarrassment to Catherine. Yet Warren had been Catherine's life, her very raison d'être. Without him, without his confusion, his immaturity, his grand, dependent schemes, she had no anchor, and was so distraught, she required hospitalization.

SEEING ONLY THE LOSS

One day, after she was out of the hospital, I ran into her and was quite taken aback by her appearance. She was wan. She was distracted. She seemed to be struggling for composure.

There was a tension in her carriage, a stiff-upper-lip quality. Being in her presence was almost exhausting. She had also lost a lot of weight. And Warren. It showed.

"Catherine," I said, "I'm glad to see you."

Immediately, she said, "I don't know how I'll manage without Warren. What am I going to do, BarBara?"

Instinctively, I wanted to take her hand. But our relationship had always been highly professional, and I wanted to monitor carefully this move into her personal life. It also concerned me that she was so emotionally raw that she started this particular conversation on the street. I suggested a quiet tea room only a block away.

She continued. "I'll have to take care of the children all by myself now. I can't do that."

I took her hand. "You've been doing it for years, Catherine." But she saw only the loss.

A LIFE IN LIMBO

I was deeply concerned about Catherine after her return to LCI. Our conversations left me with the gnawing sense that her life remained in limbo. Still, her sense of strategic marketing was as brilliant as ever.

However, the news reaching me from LCI, from the rank-and-file, and eventually from Jim Culpepper, was alarming. Catherine's very professionalism was suffering. She started arriving grossly late to meetings, without explanation or apology. However valid, her criticisms of her staff and other members of management were inappropriately public. She went through three secretaries in as many months, none of whom could locate her in a pinch.

I wanted to help Catherine. People in crisis can be counseled, get back on the track, and relocate their niche and commitment. Companies can be enormously understanding and supportive of employees who have problems. It had been a win-win situation with Catherine and LCI, and it could be again. She was back on the job, coming out of her crisis, but it was slow going. Every step forward had its compensatory, agonizing step backward. Along with her colleagues, I kept watching her groping. It seemed a terrible loss that another woman would come this close to the top and short-circuit.

JOLTED INTO AWARENESS

The day I got the call from Jim Culpepper telling me that Catherine would be fired is a day I'll never forget.

Later that very afternoon, Catherine called. "Well, Bar-Bara, let's go to it." That's all she said, but there was a surprising lilt to her voice. My spirits buoyed a little and I thought truly there was hope for salvaging her career.

I asked, "Catherine, remember the long talks we had when we first met? We talked about how much impact one individual can have and how you believed in the power of the individual. You personally have had an enormous impact so far in your career."

"I've really chased the competition all over the globe, haven't I?" she said in an upbeat tone.

"You sure have," I agreed. "You also said something which surprised me at the time. That there would soon be no need for you to become president because Warren's career would take hold soon."

"BarBara, I see now that Warren wasn't my whole life. Most of it, perhaps. My heart, certainly. But *I* built my career and I screwed it up and I can put it back together. This last year is behind me now. I have a clean slate. Let's fill it in."

During the three-month outplacement period, Catherine kept surprising me in positive ways. The shock of being fired seemed to have jolted her into awareness. She was energetic and forward-thinking. I never once saw her depressed or floundering. As for Jim and LCI, she bore no apparent bitterness. While she preferred not to dwell on her last disastrous months there, she nonetheless admitted openly that she had caused her own dismissal.

I realized that sometimes one crisis isn't enough. Sometimes it takes a second or third to clear away the self-deceptions.

POWERLESS POSITIONS

Outplacements can be depressing to do. First, there's the difficult task of rebuilding someone's self-esteem. Next, it's necessary to get the out-of-work executive to assess his or her marketability realistically and rediscover the drive to get back into the game. Finally, it's important that a few job interviews and subsequent offers happen quickly before the fragile spirits sag.

These were not my concerns about Catherine. My greatest challenge with her was guiding her through the many offers that came her way. There was a plethora of inappropriate, lesser positions being offered. Her manner made it clear that she was hardly down and out, but her firing, and LCI's superb reputation, made her prey to many organizations that otherwise would never have attempted to attract her. To date, none of our clients' needs were appropriate to Catherine's experience, but I carefully reviewed each offer she received.

Catherine was eager to return to work, and some of the offers undoubtedly looked good on the surface. I strongly encouraged her to wait, not to settle for a lesser position than she had at LCI. It was the only way to rebuild her career.

I advised Catherine to hold out, to not settle for a powerless position. She heartily agreed. Between the generous severance from LCI, her consulting work, and other investments, she could tide herself over indefinitely. Although they were now divorced, Warren was still a financial drain, but a predictable one.

THE POWER POSITION

Several weeks later I received a call from the New York headquarters of an international client. Bools & Associates had worked for a few of their regional offices. I had not worked with any of the men I would be meeting in New York. The assignment had already been vested for months with a huge recruiting firm in Manhattan, but there had been nothing approaching success. That firm was dismissed and the search would now be awarded to another executive search firm. Bools & Associates was in the running. I liked that.

The advertising agency was one of the top ten in the world, with billings of almost three billion dollars. They had sixty-three offices worldwide and were constantly adding new ones. The CEO and five corporate officers—all men—ran this company of several thousand employees. In the entire company, there was no one uniquely qualified to fill the key position I had been invited to discuss with them. They had recently created this post due to the ever more global nature of their key client's products and services being advertised to a world market. They had waited too long hoping to promote from within.

Therefore, by this time the agency was under the gun to produce a leader, someone who could put their largest client at ease, someone who would securely handle this most critical business.

The function of the job was as an international liaison linking the agency's vast network of offices in order to unify the client's advertising with transcultural messages. Their largest global client had given the agency the opportunity—actually, the charge—to build its chain of offices. All these plans might be jeopardized unless someone could harness and direct this growing phenomenon quickly. The right person could alter the very nature of the agency. The person they were looking for had to be comfortable in unfamiliar, uncharted territory, as well as a visionary who never lost focus on nuance and detail. The role *inside* the agency was one of strategic development. After the CEO, this position would carry the greatest influence and power in the agency worldwide. None of the five men in the governing and decision-making body would equal this person's power. This was a totally unique position. Never before had I seen a position created to wield so much power. Never before had I seen such a power package.

I was still catching my breath. If I could land this assignment, it would be, to this date, a position of greater magnitude than I had ever negotiated for an advertising agency. They hoped I could spend Thursday and Friday with them in New York. Oh, my God, this was Tuesday. I accepted, quickly rearranged my schedule, and left for New York the following night. I was armed with a mountain of information compiled by our research department and honed during the subsequent strategy meeting of our team in Chicago.

It had been a month of late nights, trips that consumed the weekends, and a particularly heavy workload. I had been planning to relax my schedule and coast a little. But now I was so excited I could barely sleep.

Over the next two days I met all six of the management team separately, and, finally, together. I had a two-hour break before my last meeting with the whole team. I took advantage of that time to finalize specifications on the position and do a profile of the type of person most likely to fill this job. The last meeting gave me the important opportunity to see how these men interacted, what their personal chemistry was.

I had wanted this assignment from the instant I had heard of it. My two days there, in that atmosphere, had only heightened my desire and determination to work with these people.

I was hoping to hear early the next week that Bools & Associates had been selected for the search.

I was not expecting what followed.

As I was about to leave, the CEO handed me an envelope that had captured my attention earlier in the meeting. "This should get you started, BarBara. It's the first third of your fee." I had been awarded the assignment.

Alone, in the elevator, descending from their magnificent offices, I opened the envelope. It contained the largest single check I had received to date. Best elevator thrill-ride of my life.

THEY ALL WANTED IT

Over the next four weeks I traveled to seven cities to interview ten of the final twelve candidates to emerge from our research. At this level, there is always a limited number of people who qualify—the market narrows at the top. Two of them did not need face-to-face interviews, as I had known them well for years. I eliminated three for various reasons, and one withdrew because of personal considerations that could not be overcome in time. That left us eight candidates. Eight finalists. There were six men and two women competing for this position, and they all wanted it—a lot. Catherine Ames had made the final cut.

Everyone did well. In fact, astonishingly well. In my interviews with the individuals, there had been what amounts to an exchange of efforts: I had had to convince them a little, and they, in turn, had had to convince me. It was a dance of sorts, where everyone knows the moves and steps, and, even if you want to take the lead, you each know when to relinquish it to the other to see where he or she takes you. But the music had stopped. Now we would see who the winner was. Each was determined to be that person.

EACH SHOWED PROMISE

These candidates were good. Although there were differences in their backgrounds, each showed promise of bringing excitement and innovation to this most demanding role. They were confident. There was none of the thrust and parry that had existed in my initial interviews with them. They no longer had to be convinced. Each now took on the task of convincing the men in that room that there was no better qualified candidate for that policy-making post. They all knew they were being looked at as the next leader of this vast network with global influence, and they rose to the occasion. It was a time I won't forget.

A GLOBAL OVERVIEW

Catherine was number six in the procession. For a few reasons I believed her to be one of the strongest candidates. Not all of the eight had both agency and "client side" experience— Catherine did. She was also trilingual, a definite plus. Most important, she alone had already accomplished what this post most required—unification of marketing strategies and needs on a global basis. She had helped Lincoln Foods acquire Continental, and had gone on to become international director of marketing of the merged company.

Though I knew her qualifications were on target, I was concerned about her firing, and how greatly that might affect her prospects, especially considering the other candidates' unspoiled records.

It was still unknown how well she would actually perform, how much she had really grown through her loss. I had completely reviewed the events that led to her dismissal, her relationship to her family, and how their need motivated her to great achievements. I warned the board members that she might still have these needs and she was unproven since her hospitalization. But they had been aware of her work with LCI and now saw how her skill and accomplishments fit their needs. They did extensive reference checking prior to meeting her. They understood the risk but wanted to take it. Catherine, too, knew what had caused her dismissal: her connection to her husband in an unhealthy, collusive relationship. She knew all the facts would be open for examination by any prospective employer we might introduce her to. She stated she had made the decision to function fully as an emotionally independent person and welcomed whatever scrutiny was necessary for the chance to present herself.

I wasn't prepared for the absolute rightness of Catherine's presentation. What happened was magic. She addressed her problems up front. She never made an excuse or put the responsibility on anyone but herself. She had worked up a complete family history and set of values, stating that all the women in her family made contributions to the larger society transcending their personal needs alone. Never one to dwell on problems, she kept this part short and direct and moved quickly onto the business at hand.

Catherine had built vast business resources and contacts through industry associations and, consequently, was involved in issues affecting the industry as a whole, often on a global basis. She had traveled throughout Africa studying food supplies and possible nutritional improvements. She had been involved with companies that were concerned with world issues that transcended immediate local and regional concerns. Thus, her very tone and every statement assumed a world view. She conducted herself in such a way that she was already part of the team and contributing to the advancement of their collective dream. No idea was too large in scope for them to consider. When Catherine's allotted time had expired—in fact, precisely when her allotted time had expired—Catherine completed her presentation. They didn't want to let her go. She had electrified the room.

DESTINED FOR THE TOP

It was tough on the last two candidates: After Catherine, their presentations seemed anticlimactic. While the agency management behaved properly and showed genuine interest—they were too professional to do otherwise—the thrill was gone. Catherine had won the job.

Catherine followed up the next day with an assumptive move that clearly indicated both her commitment and confidence: She requested to meet the international client. I advised the board against this premature step. Should they decide to involve their client at this point anyway, I suggested the number two and three choices be included. But two days later the board voted Catherine alone was to meet their client. I absolutely knew she had the job. But candidates should not generally be introduced to an agency's clients unless the client is part of the process to attract these candidates or the individual is already on the team. A move like this has been known to backfire.

Soon thereafter, Catherine did indeed meet the international client. He had a similar response to that of the board of directors. Here was indeed a person he could trust to lead his account as well as keep his agency resources strong. Catherine had satisfied and gained the confidence of two separate groups whose needs were different but whose goals were allied. This was a woman clearly destined for the top. Again!

The next week a formal offer was extended in principle. A pride of lawyers met to work out the details of the contract. I mediated. The final package contained thirty-two components for a total compensation approaching seven figures. It was iron-clad for a three-year minimum guarantee. Perks were abundant: private schooling abroad for the children and travel on the Concorde for Catherine. Everything was in place. It was just a matter of Catherine signing the document. As Catherine knew, protocol called for her to return the contract within three or four days.

She was about to control more than $3 billion in revenues and several thousand employees worldwide. She would be the only one in this organization positioned to succeed the CEO. She now had only to do her job.

POWER FAILURE

Then something quite unexpected happened. Catherine disappeared.

For three days she could not be located anywhere. She didn't return calls left on her answering machine. No one knew where she might be. Her daughter Emma didn't even know where her mother was. On the fourth day I tried Emma again. She still didn't know where Catherine was. Just as I was about to hang up, Emma casually remarked that her mother had packed a few things and gone off with Zeke. *Zeke?*

Later that day Catherine reappeared, only to announce that she was declining the position. Instead, she would be accepting the presidency of a small ten-million-dollar agency in the Midwest. She included another announcement: She and Zeke had married.

My first thought was that Zeke had a Midwest-based career, and in a conventional sense of a wife's place, Catherine chose her location based on his. I could barely contain my anger that she had never mentioned this critical new element in her life that clearly affected our complex negotiations.

Then I learned the startling truth—Zeke's business had major offices in both New York and London, and he was never in the Midwest. What could this possibly be about? Had Catherine accepted the international post, they could have coordinated many, if not most, of their activities. Now, with her new job, they would hardly ever see each other. Clearly, Zeke's location had nothing to do with her decision.

As for the job she accepted, it could not compare to the position she turned down. It was a small, regional agency. Good people, but limited scope. A much smaller job than the one she'd had at LCI. A ridiculously small job and one that could not possibly have paid more than a quarter of the compensation compared to this current offer.

My clients in New York and I were totally confused. To my knowledge, no one had ever turned down such an opportunity. Actually, such an opportunity had never existed to be turned down.

"NO MORE FEMALES"

I had been working with Catherine for a long time and vowed never to work with her again—how could I? How could I recommend someone that erratic?

The worst blow was still to come.

My work wasn't over. The powerful international position remained unfilled. In a hectic few days I had pulled together my backup strategies, proposed offers for the remaining finalists, and phoned my client. Their second choice had been significantly promoted in the intervening week and a half, and was no longer available. Their subsequent choices included two men and a woman. I recommended they inform their client immediately and tell them they were ready to make offers to others as qualified and capable as Catherine.

My clients agreed, but the CEO interrupted with a caveat. This chief executive, who had previously been so unbiased and straightforward, said to me in the most disheartened and exhausted tone, "No more females, BarBara. We just don't have the time."

I thought to myself, the next time someone said, "Why did a man get that job when there are women more qualified?" I would scream. Because it was often my frustrating, painful, heartbreaking experience that women more qualified *were* offered the job.

And like Catherine, turned it down.

LIVING A LIE

I don't know when it struck me, but all of Catherine's personal failures and tragedies were very public. Catherine didn't just have a setback in her level of performance in the wake of a divorce, she was *hospitalized*. She didn't just get demoted or edged out, she was *fired*. She *begged* to be fired. Her underperforming husband occupied an office for all her co-workers to see and whisper about. Her son was found dead and she hurried back to work.

I remember a classic tenet of psychology: If someone lives a lie, there is likely to be an outward manifestation. Catherine could stand before the world—cool, brilliant, professional— while everything about her personal life was crying out for help.

What everyone, including myself, failed to realize at the time was that her entrepreneurial, risk-taking bent was not fully grounded in her own personal substance and sense of self-worth. Rather, it was made possible by her very inability to see the truthful situation of her own life.

Catherine had been offered one incredible opportunity to put her career and her life back on track. More than that, she was offered real power.

Catherine Ames's functioning at a level below her true ability is, sadly, a loss for all of us. In her innovative cross-national, cross-cultural business dealings, Catherine exhibited a talent for global community. With the LCI merger she had successfully united two anxious and competing companies into a cohesive and productive whole. Her international dealings also displayed her absolute win-win philosophy, and were possible owing to her creative abilities in simultaneously minimizing differences, meeting needs, and maximizing unique contributions. Such an asset to the global business community! Tragically, Catherine's Power Failure not only limited the scope of her own life and her children's lives, but denied the world one more effective vehicle for peaceful communication and interaction.

She was a maverick because she had a wonderful time playing at her career. Somehow, it never occurred to her that her career was also a part of her real life.

Today, as I write this, Catherine is out of work.

Not only out of work, but untouchable. Not because of her one-time firing or reports of her performance problems or absenteeism during her last few months at LCI, but because of her poor judgment in taking a job so far beneath her. Although fewer than a dozen people ever knew about her truly powerful opportunity, it was clear to all that she could have secured a position more in keeping with the level of her ability than being in a ten-million-dollar agency. (Imagine one of the Armours opening a hot-dog stand.) She destroyed her credibility, and leaders must be credible.

IN THE WAKE OF PERSONAL CRISIS

It must be made clear that Catherine's personal crises *alone* did not ostracize her from her industry. Many people in top management have also undergone temporary setbacks in the wake of personal crisis. A crisis can be forgiven because, by definition, it is a temporary period of intense change and readjustment. People who are not destroyed by it usually emerge stronger and more well-rounded.

Catherine's career is, today, not viable because she made a deadly professional move. People who surmount crisis are sometimes welcomed back. People who make bad decisions—publicly bad decisions—are poison.

HER INTERNAL SCRIPT

On one hand, Catherine really focused on her business and the issues therein. On the other, she was waiting for her man to give direction to her life. In the short run, she could allow herself to succeed, even thrive, on that very success. But in the long run, she needed to create a self-deception in her marriage and her relationship with family in order not to confront that very visible success. Was it also true that in order to support her elaborate deception she had to be with a man who was intellectually and even physically powerful but substantively weak?

Her relational needs had totally blinded her to the situational reality of her life. Her interior view of her family structure and her service-oriented role in it were at odds with the truth of her real-world power and influence. From a career and power standpoint, the people and roles in Catherine's internal script represented a wall she didn't even know she had to scale.

NEEDING TO BE NEEDED

Catherine had incredible focus on her career when her man or her family was in need. As long as that situation prevailed, the career received the total emphasis it required. But to sustain that pace, that very intense focus, those who depended on her must never succeed—or, in the case of her first husband and son, leave her—because she would then be left doing it all for herself. Alone. Without needy, hurting people to be successful *for,* Catherine lost her vision, her drive, her need. Without ongoing and highly visible trauma to push her forward, she could make only destructive choices. As it turned out, Zeke was a very powerful man who wanted to take care of her. Her inconsequential career choice was only a glimmer of what was left of *her.*

FAR-REACHING CONSEQUENCES

Catherine's bad decision had far-reaching consequences. The agency that Catherine turned down was able to placate their global client, but only for a short time. The man who took the job instead was very competent, but the client felt disappointed by Catherine's absence. No one else was truly like her. Within months the agency lost the account, and shortly thereafter was merged.

Today it's just one more giant agency without a heart or point of view. Its people are entrenched in layers of management and are growing restless.

I felt as if I were watching the sad half of the classic film *It's a Wonderful Life.* Catherine's presence in that agency would have had worldwide impact—her absence was keenly felt.

And the women at the agency all suffered. Mergers create more top management, all men, and put men and women alike in upper middle management even further from the top. Hence the July 1986 quote in *Madison Avenue:* "A woman has virtually no chance of ever heading a megamerged agency."

There are two probable scenarios had Catherine assumed

the position offered to her, both positive. The agency might have remained in private ownership, and its thousands of people would have benefited. Or, had Catherine decided to merge the agency, she would have become the first—and to date the only—woman to head a megamerged agency. And as an international unifying force, it is not difficult to envision Catherine's influence on the entire industry.

Not only did Catherine suffer loss, thousands of employees were affected adversely. On a cultural level, Catherine's actions were a message both to and about the American woman. To quote Clare Boothe Luce:

> Because I am a woman, I must make unusual efforts to succeed. If I fail, no one will say, "She doesn't have what it takes," they will say, "women don't have what it takes."

Catherine Ames could easily have been at the very top. She might have been a role model, a pinnacle of hope, a legendary pioneer for generations of American businesswomen to follow.

Instead, many women are bailing out. The difficult climb is still ahead of us, and the top policy-making spots still elusive. When I experience an open-minded client's *new* antiwoman bias, the words "no more females, BarBara, we just don't have the time" keep ringing in my ears.

Today, years later, there is still no woman running any of the country's largest advertising agencies. According to *Advertising Age,* an industry bible, there's not likely to be one. In my view, it could be a decade. There are none on the horizon. *Madison Avenue* continues, "It would take a superwoman of as yet unidentified and unobserved ability to stand a ghost of a chance of running a megamerged male bastion."

Catherine Ames had that chance—and committed Power Failure.

▪ ▪ ▪

We understand Maria Stollenwerk and how her father's needs became her destiny.

Vicki Dennison's perspective was determined on a constantly shifting horizon by the needs and logisitical deployment of the army.

Mary Louise DeVaney's path was cleared of obstacles, but the road signs were unmarked and the destination had no name.

Catherine Ames broke all the rules as long as they were somebody else's.

And then there is Sandy Auerbach, who was convinced the rules didn't require breaking—how could they? They didn't apply to her—for she had a piece of the future.

SANDY AUERBACH

∎

She thought it was forever, but she hadn't read the fine print.

WHEN SUSAN announced, "BarBara, it's Sandy Auerbach on line seven," I experienced a duality of feelings. In the back of my mind, on an almost subconscious level, I had been anticipating this call for months, ever since Sandy had refused to interview for a position with Drake Communications, the electronics conglomerate. *Now* she was calling, and for Sandy, her timing was all wrong. I had tried to make her understand the explosive nature of her situation. But she was unable to accept what I had said and now it was too late.

Sandy had been fired. She wanted to come talk to me.

A PERSONAL MISSION

It had been years since Sandy, with her newly minted MBA from Washington University, had accepted a position with Norman and Dearborn, a medium-size packaged-goods corporation. It was based in St. Louis, and only a few of its scores of brands enjoyed national distribution. Even though Sandy had been offered trainee positions in much larger and more established firms, she later told me that three things had absolutely attracted her to Norman and Dearborn: they were hungry, they were ethical, and there was room at the top.

I often find that the most exciting and dynamic executives of either sex have some sort of personal mission. More than simply attending to the bottom line, they use their business careers as a vehicle to express some personal belief, to "make a difference," or to "change things for the better." In short, they have personal power. Often, an individual can articulate the mission, and his or her enthusiasm will motivate and unite others.

Sandy expressed her mission in terms of "business responsiveness." In my first meeting with her, when she had just become an assistant brand manager, she explained that her belief in "the need for business to be more responsive" was threefold: more responsive to consumers, more responsive to retailers and suppliers, and more responsive to employees. "We *talk* to the public through our products," she said. "And we have to meet the needs of the grocers, so we'll be more clearly heard."

THEY NEVER WANTED TO PART WITH HER

That credo of responsiveness was Sandy's hallmark from her start at Norman and Dearborn. She had entered in sales, and traveled endlessly and relentlessly. While others complained about never being home, Sandy wanted to know where else she could go. Every encounter with store personnel turned into a question-and-answer period for Sandy. She wanted to know exactly what they wanted from Norman and Dearborn's products and product line. What were the complaints their customers made? What were the customers looking for? What would make their lives easier? How could Norman and Dearborn help? While competing salespeople were always fighting for better frontings and shelf space (and hoping for better territories), Sandy's lengthy and genuine interest in the needs of the grocers gained her products ideal shelf space and frontings as if by fiat. Whenever she came back to the home office, she wasted no time in reporting all her insights in memo form and getting those memos the fullest possible readership by management, marketing, and research and development.

When she wasn't on the road, she was all over Norman and Dearborn. Catapulted by sheer ambition, she volunteered for every tough assignment that came along. While others hid in their offices, Sandy went looking for work. Soon a trend developed in Sandy's career: Management started asking for her on a particular brand. Once exposed to her, her drive, her mind, and her strong point of view, they never wanted to part with her.

SEEING ONLY OPPORTUNITY

Jealous rumors soon surfaced that Sandy got "all the creamy assignments." In truth, Sandy was consistently put into troubled areas because she performed magnificently. When others saw a situation as "between a rock and a hard place," Sandy saw only opportunity. Her visibility soared with every new success. In a remarkably brief span (eight years of hard work and noticeable profits), Sandy shot to the position of marketing director for the grocery products division of Norman and Dearborn.

■ ■ ■

NOT A MEDIA HEROINE

Interestingly, Sandy never became a public spokeswoman for the corporation, as often happens with women nearing the top. She had never been interested in public speaking and steadfastly refused to discuss any particulars of her personal life, which much of the media clamored for. There was nothing special about Sandy's appearance. She was rather small with light brown hair worn in an undistinguished style that fell over her eyes and looked in need of a trim. She wore horn-rimmed glasses that were too big for her small face. Sandy spent no time in the glare of publicity and all her time furthering Norman and Dearborn's products in the manner at which she was expert.

Although Sandy never became a media heroine, she was a clear role model for many young women (and men) at Norman and Dearborn.

Her staff loved her. One of her senior managers described the situation to me this way: "We're not equal to her in the hierarchy—I mean, we know where we fit in the 'corporate family,' I dare say. But with Sandy, our ideas are equal, always considered, and she's never, ever arbitrary. Her actions make sense to us because, so often, we have developed them together, and for that she always gives credit where credit is due. I guess the big thing is, there's a sense with most of us in the division that we keep building something, and it's fun. You never feel like you're wasting your time. Of course, Sandy wouldn't let you."

Sandy was a joy to recruit for. Her management skills were becoming well known (but never as successfully duplicated). When I would contact candidates to work for Norman and Dearborn, I got used to their asking; "Is it in Sandy Auerbach's division?" If my answer was yes, the process was noticeably quickened and much more often successful.

■   ■   ■

THE MAN WHO OWNS MORNING

As she progressed within Norman and Dearborn, it was only natural she would be spending more time with Tom Roman. Tom was president of the grocery products division and a center of innovation at the corporation. His influence was felt throughout Norman and Dearborn, not only for his own areas of expertise but for what he engendered in all the divisions.

Unlike Sandy, Tom had built his ascent on just one piece of business—one of his own creation. However, it was Norman and Dearborn's most visible and profitable product, and a new-product case study. He had gone against the prevailing wisdom to force the introduction of a menthol soap.

Tom insisted it be named A.M., the Menthol Soap. The test commercial for A.M. had been watched over and produced by Norman and Dearborn's advertising agency for new products. But like everything else about A.M., it had been primarily designed and developed by Tom Roman.

It was unprecedented for a new entry into the brand-loyal personal soap category to become the largest-selling deodorant soap in four years' time.

Tom then introduced a frozen pancake mix that was microwaveable, followed by a pulp-heavy orange juice. In no time at all Tom was known as the Man Who Owns Morning.

WORKAHOLICS

Evenings usually found Tom at work. And Tom usually found Sandy at the office as well. Sandy and Tom were both workaholics. Their work, and their working hours, forced them to spend more and more time together. They both had solid visions about their work and their industry. They both cared passionately about the products they developed and represented. They were meant for each other. They realized they were falling in love. Tom was fifteen years older than Sandy. He had never been married and had come to think that he never would be. Sandy hadn't given it a great deal of thought; besides, there was plenty of time. So they got married in a simple, no-nonsense ceremony that befitted the two of them.

They were back to work on Monday.

LOVED BY CONSUMERS—AND WALL STREET

Over the next few years Norman and Dearborn experienced huge expansion. A.M. and the other "morning products," along with Sandy's "business responsiveness" ethic was proving to be an unbeatable combination. Norman and Dearborn was becoming beloved by consumers and Wall Street. These were heady times, as Sandy and Tom were swept along on the momentum of innovation.

During these years Sandy and Tom also started a family. In fact, they had twins, and shared equally in parenting. Sandy, who had been comfortably raised with sitters, felt she was skilled at hiring a nurturing and responsible housekeeper. Sandy and Tom also felt it was absolutely necessary for children to feel at home with more than one person.

From the beginning—when the twins were still infants—Sandy and Tom each had one of the babies strapped to their chests. They perceived themselves as balanced in home and work.

Meanwhile, Mr. Dearborn, the CEO of Norman and Dearborn, became something of a national figure. Finally, he was happy to assume the mantle of spokesman for a new generation of products and a new conscience that had developed among the mass-merchandisers. Besides, the tedious day-today running of Norman and Dearborn had never been more efficient than it was under Tom Roman's steady, and now seasoned hand. In effect, Roman and Dearborn were running Norman and Dearborn in tandem. In reality, Roman and Auerbach were running Norman and Dearborn, while Dearborn became the "corporate crown" and waved to the grateful crowds.

Dearborn assumed the chairman of the board title, and the board of directors unanimously elected Tom Roman to be the new CEO.

Sandy was promoted to president of her division. She promoted one of her lieutenants—a bright and personable man some years her senior, whom she had recruited with my help—to marketing director. Norman and Dearborn was running very lean and had minimal top management structure. This was partly because of the rapid and explosive growth, and partly because Tom was retaining as much control as possible himself, to orchestrate the company's growth.

Sandy and Tom each worked stunningly long hours, and seemed to thrive on it. She told me they often gave the housekeeper Saturdays off and brought the kids into the office with them.

They were a vital and powerful corporate family.

A DARK CONSEQUENCE

At the time, things couldn't have seemed rosier. Sandy Auerbach was a dedicated professional on the rise. She also had a full and happy personal life. I was glad to know her, and respected her. I had recruited many of her senior staffers, and admired her business ethics and unique management abilities. Her very credo of "responsiveness" and her high-touch, "we're-all-in-this-together" management style seemed to have a slightly feminine quality.

Everything about her life seemed to be a blueprint for women in corporate life.

Later, however, another aspect of Sandy's roots would result in a dark consequence. As with the other women in this book, I later came to believe that Sandy's underlying *relationalism* could blind her to a difficult situation and negate her personal power.

In my many conversations with Sandy over the years of our business relationship, I had come to understand a great deal about her family—both past and present.

A LIFESCRIPT PLAYED AGAIN

Sandy, single, career-focused, and undeniably independent throughout her twenties, seemed to be recreating an advanced version of the Auerbach family setup from the fifties when she agreed to marry Tom Roman a month after her thirty-second birthday.

I'm often amazed how successfully someone can resist the old family script for years and then find oneself in a remarkably similar situation. Maggie Scarf comments on this phenomenon in *Intimate Partners:*

> Partners who married expecting to live happily ever after frequently find themselves in dilemmas that bear some eerie resemblance to one or both spouses' earlier experiences in the family environment.
>
> How does it happen, so routinely, that we ignore the organic connection between a couple's present relationship and the individual history of each of the partners?
>
> We seem to be uncannily *efficient* when it comes to choosing partners who will help us get into situa-

tions that recapitulate earlier dilemmas that have never been successfully mastered. It is as if we were guided by a dizzyingly complex and yet remarkably precise internalized radar.

"FOR THE GOOD OF YOUR FATHER'S PRACTICE"

Sandy's parents had built a dental practice into a thriving business that employed several other dentists as junior partners and associates.

At first the office consisted of just Dr. Auerbach's lone degree from dental college. Sandy's parents worked hard and never lost sight of their goal. Sandy came along at an inconvenient time, and they all used to joke that the day Mrs. Auerbach's water broke was blessedly free from any other emergencies and Dr. Auerbach was able to take her to the hospital, which was only a mile and a half away.

Mrs. Auerbach was back at work three weeks later, and even though she had wanted to breastfeed Sandy, that was but the first of many compromises that were made, "for the good of your father's practice."

So Sandy learned to drink from baby bottles and grew accustomed to the frequent changes of housekeepers and babysitters and, best yet, was sometimes allowed to spend the day at her father's office.

She helped her mother however she could, because her mother was the receptionist and office manager as well as psychologist, cleaning lady, bookkeeper, and keeper of the flame under the coffeepot.

On Wednesdays, when Sandy's father played golf, Sandy's mother would catch up on the bookkeeping and pray there would be no emergencies. Sandy, on the other hand, *wanted* emergencies because she loved the excitement and it was the only time she saw her mother take charge at the office. As she grew older it meant she could drive and go find her father on the golf course.

Sandy adored her father, who was very sophisticated and a little pompous. (Sandy told me, "That can be appealing when it isn't used against you.") She loved it when they went out to eat and he would make reservations as "Dr. Auerbach and party." But in many ways, Sandy was more like her mother: hardworking, a whiz-bang at details, no task too menial, and always ready to step in and take charge.

HIS NAME ON THE DOOR

People endeavor to take in traits and knowledge from both parents. In truth, both parents serve as role models for their children of either sex.

In many households of the last generation, women grew up with head-of-household fathers and powerless housewife/mothers. Sandy Auerbach had a mother who simultaneously fit this pattern and broke it.

She broke it by being capable, confident, and the backbone of the family's dental practice. Sandy grew up believing that women's efforts were productive and profitable, that women were indispensable in making a business work.

Lucille Auerbach fit the pattern by always presenting herself "in deference to" her husband. Sandy's father was the head of the household and the head of the practice. *His* skills, education, and status were necessary for the business to exist at all. *He* was the line player, the one with his name on the door.

This fact was not lost on Sandy. She told me that her mother was the one who made the place profitable, who worked the long hours, who pulled the practice through hard times. Yet whenever patients were present (and after a while when they were not), Sandy's mother called her husband "Dr. Auerbach," while he called her "Lucille."

MOTHERS AND DAUGHTERS

With the expanding opportunities for women over the last two decades since the women's movement began, many women saw a way out—if not for themselves, then for their daughters. Often these mothers wanted the very independence for their daughters that they themselves had been denied. Many successful women report tremendous encouragement and support from their mothers.

To a point.

And where does that support and encouragement break down?

In the novel *Blue Rise,* psychiatrist Rebecca Hill tells us of a woman who is, at thirty-five, still trying to separate herself from her mother's approved script, and make choices outside the family repertoire:

> [My mother] is busy specializing in the past and I come to her bearing the future and say, "Tell me I have a right to save myself. Tell me you know what I'm talking about. Admit that your life and all that pain were for nothing."
>
> She is aghast. I was always supposed to live a better life than she did. "Don't do what I did," she has said. But the catch was, "If you don't do what I did, how will I know you as my daughter?"

■ ■ ■

FATHERS AND DAUGHTERS

And what does a daughter learn from her father? In a culture where the roles are split, the message often is, too. Like with Mother, Father may say psychologically, "Grow up, but don't leave home."

Within each father is a little boy who had the childhood experience of being raised first and foremost by a woman. Some psychologists postulate that men's desire to control and dominate women has its roots in the toddlerhood scenario described in the chapter, "The Phenomenon of Power Failure": being told that they are "not like mother" at a time when she is the only psychological "other" is experienced as a profound betrayal. At a deep subconscious level, men need to bring women close, and yet feel it is dangerous to do so. From an anthropological point of view, Patricia McBroom has this to say regarding Peggy Sanday's "cross-cultural analysis of more than one hundred societies":

> A sexual division of labor that removes men from
> taking a nurturant role promotes a masculine ethos
> focused upon domination and war.

A man with a daughter has temporarily healed the old wound. For many years of her childhood he finally has control of an adoring female who cannot leave him. He endeavors to bring her close and delights in teaching her what he knows.

But the emerging reality of her adolescence reopens the scar he incurred and repressed as a toddler—that of mother leaving before *he* was ready to separate. His first close relationship was irrevocably severed by *her,* and it threatens to happen again. So the adult male vacillates—as a toddler would—between the defense mechanisms of seduction and angry withdrawal, which serves only to convince a young girl who does not yet have her independence that obtaining it is a very dangerous endeavor.

SOMETHING WAS BROKEN

For Sandy, this message started coming through loud and clear when she was in high school.

Sandy had consistently arranged her schedule in high school so she could be free Wednesday afternoons to help her mother at her father's office. How she loved those occasions when circumstances dictated the hurried rush to the country club, the deliberate parking in the tow-away zone, and her father's obvious pride in announcing, "Here comes my daughter, Sandy. There must be an emergency."

Sandy knew she was just a messenger. But, oh, how she loved the message.

One Wednesday, Sandy had a meeting of the Science Club at 3:00 and didn't go into the dental office. She was to deliver a paper and couldn't, or wouldn't, miss it. That was the same afternoon that Sonny Fitzsimmons was examining his new catcher's mitt as he rode his bike down Fourth Avenue and ran into the back of a truck that stopped suddenly. Sonny hit the locking mechanism on the truck's rear doors and lost seven teeth in the process.

While Sandy gave her science report, her mother sent a young technician to the country club to retrieve Dr. Auerbach.

Sonny's broken teeth were fixed, but something else was not. Dr. Auerbach announced to his daughter that since he could no longer count on her readiness every Wednesday, he would obtain a beeper.

Sandy told me she missed going to the golf course Wednesday afternoons. She also told me, after that, she had Wednesday afternoons to herself. She had lost interest in the Science Club.

HIDING A CAPACITY FOR ADULTHOOD

On a subconscious level, a father defends himself against his daughter's leaving by threatening to leave first. (Metaphorically, obtaining a beeper could be an establishment of emotional distance.) *She* defends herself against the possibility of his leaving by abandoning or hiding—at least psychologically—her strivings for independence and capacity for adulthood.

A PSYCHOLOGICAL CATCH-22

Like most executive women currently in their twenties, thirties, or forties, Sandy was undoubtedly trying to keep the best of what she learned from each of her parents and discard what was no longer adaptive. However, a relational orientation *was* femininity in the fifties, when Sandy was still, first and foremost, a daughter.

How is a "daughter" to achieve the personal power and independence her mother never had and still be recognizable to her? How is a "daughter" to express the strength and determination she learned from her father yet remain an "adoring"—and unthreatening—female?

Given this subconscious Catch-22, what, then, is a bright, articulate, capable young woman to do? In short, how can she be a modern executive and a traditional woman at the same time?

One answer might be to marry the CEO.

AN UNDERLYING RELATIONAL ORIENTATION

Of course, there might be a much more mundane explanation for Sandy's marriage to Tom. They spent a lot of time together, they shared the same goals—what better basis for a romance? It seemed like an eighties fairy tale: two independent, hardworking professionals meet, make money, and make love. All the while, of course, retaining their independent goals and aspirations.

In retrospect, however, I absolutely question Sandy's psychological separateness. Despite her personal achievements and independent status, this thirty-two-year-old woman was waiting for the day when she could experience herself *in relation to* a successful, goal-oriented man. Although at the time I didn't understand the full import of the following conversation, I now believe it to be an indicator of Sandy's underlying relational orientation.

Shortly after their marriage, I took Sandy to lunch to celebrate. Of course, I had asked them both to lunch, but Tom was speaking at a marketing symposium at Wharton. I asked Sandy how work had changed since she and Tom had been married—if it was making a difference, and, if so, how?

Sandy laughed. "No difference at work. In fact, the biggest difference is that I finally got around to changing my driver's license and dentist."

"Would you care to elaborate? I'm afraid I'm not following."

"Well, my license has always been at my parents' address in Pennsylvania. So I go home every Thanksgiving and Dad checks my teeth. And every three years I get my license renewed. Once I married Tom, I thought I should finally do something about this." She reached down and unzipped her handbag and removed a tan leather Day-Timer wallet. She located her driver's license and proudly held it out for me to see. Her smiling photo beamed at me.

"See? I'm finally a Missourian. And my dentist is only a block from the office—he's an old college friend of Tom's."

Clearly, for Sandy, adulthood was reached by switching allegiances. She had graduated from being a daughter. She was now a wife.

Sandy Auerbach felt she had lucked into life when she shared a bed, a name, and the future of a corporation with the same man. She was married to the CEO *and* the corporation in the same breath. For Sandy, the personal and professional became so inextricably fused and confused that she was unable to assess the reality of her work situation.

A BAD SITUATION

Norman and Dearborn's record growth had created legitimate needs for top quality executives at every level. Specifically, they needed stronger people at Sandy's level to head the other four divisions. There were also two openings on the ten-person board of directors.

Sandy was clearly in place to be elected to a seat on the board. But there were delays. The board suddenly gave voice to the rumors of a merger and they "could not possibly afford to make any more management changes at present." They had to move carefully. Wait and see.

I knew this lull was slow death for Sandy. I knew a couple of other things as well. Sandy's peers—the other four division presidents—were not as sharp as she was for a very good reason: Norman and Dearborn could not attract or keep top talent in management positions ever since Sandy's and Tom's remarkable ascents. It had become one of the most exciting companies around and one that everyone in the industry was speculating about and watching very carefully, but—and this is a very big "but"—no one on the outside wanted to work there. Everyone was convinced they would be locked out by Sandy and Tom's relationship. No one wanted to invest his or her career in a corporation where it was perceived no career prospects existed for anyone but the Romans. Word had gone out that open competition with Sandy would be resented by Tom, and that Sandy, only in her late thirties, would never leave Norman and Dearborn.

At least not by choice.

"WE'RE GOING TO HAVE TO MAKE SOME CHANGES"

Mr. Dearborn called me at our offices one day and commenced a long and rather rambling conversation that made little cognitive sense to me. I had not spoken at length with the man before, and was beginning to assume this was his personal style, when he turned a verbal corner and his objective was revealed.

"We're going to have to make some changes, BarBara, and I'll need your discreet help."

"What are the reasons for the changes?" I asked him cautiously.

"Growth." He answered. "You know how dramatic our growth has been."

"Given that *you* called me, Mr. Dearborn, these changes must be in top management." This was not a man who was easy to pin down.

"As you're aware, BarBara, we are running very lean. We are experiencing some difficulties in attracting the people we want."

"I've been aware of that."

"The people who have brought us to this point," he continued, "sadly appear to be inhibiting our future."

"Do I understand you correctly, Mr. Dearborn, that this is an assignment you're giving me?" I believed I *more* than understood. But I wanted to hear him say it.

"The assignment is yours, if you understand it correctly. I'll have Carl Hendler call you. Good-bye, BarBara, I'm glad we've had this talk."

Although Dearborn had carefully avoided specifics, his covert message was: "Sandy must go." If I doubted that for a minute, the subsequent call from Carl "Hatchet Man" Hendler made it only too clear.

Toward the end of our conversation I proselytized for the inherent dignity of direct communication with Sandy and Tom about this unworkable situation.

"Carl, has the board considered telling Sandy and Tom the problem their situation has created?"

"We have no problem with *Tom,*" Carl answered. "And we can't afford to lose him." He was very matter-of-fact.

"Then may I suggest you talk to Sandy directly?" I attempted.

"Sandy is Tom's responsibility," was his immediate reply.

"WE'D HIRE HER IN A MINUTE"

In subsequent conversations with Mr. Dearborn and Carl Hendler it became increasing clear that Sandy was not only "Tom's responsibility," but was fast becoming mine as well. They both assumed it would be easy for me to find her a suitable position elsewhere. Dearborn referred to her as "presidential material." Hendler said, "Hell, BarBara, *we'd* hire her in a minute."

They were well aware of Sandy's drive, focus, abilities, and experience. They were also aware that at Norman and Dearborn she was blocked. Were it either of them, they would absolutely consider another company.

What they didn't realize was that Sandy would not.

NOT BELIEVING THE PROBLEM

I told Sandy how well-respected she was in the industry, and that two other major corporations had asked me about her and requested my arranging meetings between them. I also suggested she consider moving to an advertising agency where her innovative skills would be a tremendous asset.

She listened. She loved the suggestions and complimented me for my willingness to suggest the untried. She even made superb recommendations of other people suitable for these positions. It just wasn't for her.

"I know where I want to be, BarBara, and that's right where I am. They've been so good to me here, I don't think I'll ever want to leave. They've earned my loyalty. Sure, they could move faster, but hasn't that always been my problem?" She laughed because we both understood her impatience with the norm. And then came the clincher.

"I could never truly consider a position where I might be competing with *Tom.*" She paused, and then, with somewhat more intensity: "Tom and I are a *team,* BarBara."

And Sandy *refused to believe* Norman and Dearborn had a problem attracting senior people to the organization. I was as emphatic and specific as I could be and still maintain discretion. But Sandy was emotionally blocked. "BarBara, I'm afraid you're buying the rumors, and they're unfounded. The board would have told me." She amended that. "Tom would have told me."

Tom never discussed this with Sandy because the board never discussed it with Tom. And certainly not with Sandy. But it was open discussion behind their backs. They were afraid of losing Tom—he controlled the biggest and most visible piece of Norman and Dearborn's business. There was no one who could possibly take his place. They simply could not afford his departure.

PERFECT FOR SANDY

Three months passed and nothing changed at Norman and Dearborn. I decided to give it another shot with Sandy. Specifically, I had a client—Drake Communications, the electronics conglomerate—who was interested in Sandy for their director of marketing post that was about to open up. It could, in all probability, lead to the presidency. They were an astonishingly progressive and very aggressive company who had been on a rampage of acquisitions. Two other facts about Drake were perfect for Sandy: Their product line in no way competed with Norman and Dearborn's and they were based in St. Louis.

Sandy wouldn't even meet. And when confronted again with "the problem," she made excuses for why Norman and Dearborn's senior management recruitment efforts continued to fail.

I was shocked. As we talked, it was clear she had a sense of loyalty ("completeness," she called it) to Norman and Dearborn that superseded her loyalty to herself. That superseded her better judgment. She behaved as if Norman and Dearborn were her family, not her company. The situation wasn't good.

Trust, loyalty, and integrity merge as issues here. In *Breaking into the Boardroom,* Jinx Melia states:

> The currency most valued by high-risk power brokers is loyalty. There is a significant difference in our society between female and male loyalty. Women generally operate with what we call "mar-

riage" loyalty. We will be loyal for ever and ever and ever, but only on condition that . . . (With us making the conditions). Men are more apt to use "football" loyalty; they will be loyal unconditionally, even unto death, but only today. Tomorrow the loyalty must be renegotiated.

WHAT WAS BEST FOR HER CAREER

Sandy Auerbach was a fast-track woman who stated she wanted power but would not do what was best for her career. Relational assumptions stood firmly in the way of her seeing the very dangerous situation her career was then in.

INVOKING THE RULE BOOK

Finally, it came to pass that Norman and Dearborn merged with the much larger Sentry Industries.

And Sentry Industries had been founded on Sentry Soap, their first product and the image on which their place in the history of America had been built. It wasn't much of a competitor to A.M., the Menthol Soap, but it had never been anything less than the very hook on which Sentry Industries was hung. Sacrificing A.M. to keep Sentry was not a case of good business. It was a case of paying homage to a more simple time.

A.M., the Menthol Soap was sold to another packaged-goods company—a future-looking and aggressive competitor.

Something else came with the merger: Sentry Industries' company manual. And buried deep within it was a nepotism clause:

> To avoid the appearance of impropriety, and to
> ensure no conflict of interest, or hints of favoritism,
> no relatives by birth or marriage will be hired.

Though the clause said nothing specifically concerning people already working there, the board of directors sensed an opportunity. What had been a sticky situation—a problem that had caused difficulties in hiring that could be transferred to Sentry Industries—could now be recast as one of simple rules and regulations. What they had been unable to do before could now be done by invoking the rulebook.

Tom and Sandy finally took the vacation/honeymoon that they had never had time for before. When they returned to work, Sandy was called into the boardroom, without Tom present, and fired.

Sandy was devastated.

MEN PLAY BY THE RULES

Tom was wounded. And careful. He was CEO of Sentry Industries, but he had just lost the product he had developed and grown with. It was a newly merged company, and he no longer knew everyone by name, as he had when it was just the people from Norman and Dearborn. In his mind it just wasn't a good time to take a stand. Or make a move. It wasn't good strategy.

He did not protest Sandy's firing.

Now Sandy felt doubly betrayed.

She had expected Tom to come along on his white horse and save the day. Save her. But he acted *situationally*. She acted *relationally*. They were both in character.

Sandy visited me at our offices. We discussed all of it and mapped out a game plan for (what was left of) her career. At one point she burst into tears. She told me she cried "a lot lately." And then there was a long moment of silence. I watched a dozen emotions play across her face. A hardness settled in around her mouth, and a determination was lighted in her eyes.

"BarBara, I have learned a valuable lesson here. And I have come to a conclusion."

I thought about her intense loyalty to Norman and Dearborn, the years of her talent invested there. I thought about the offers she had turned down to stay there. I remembered the times I had felt so at home in a business situation, that leaving—even to develop professionally—felt like leaving home. I thought of the board of directors who had so carefully choreographed this life-blow and the cowardly way they implemented it. Sandy's loyalty and hard work and dedication meant nothing to them in the face of their needs. I believed that she was seeing the situation that had been clear to me for some time now, and that I had tried to make clear to her. I thought for sure she would say she would never put loyalty to an organization above loyalty to herself. I was ready for her comment. Or so I thought.

"BarBara, I will never again let a man do this to me."

I cringed. A man! She hadn't learned how to assess the game any more clearly, or play it any better. She learned only, again, how much it can hurt. She still saw the problem as one of relationships. Of loyalty and betrayal.

And because she saw it that way, so did everyone else. Because there had been public tears, public tears were what everyone else had seen. Or heard about. Whereas Sandy had once been a sought-after candidate for many top power-positions, now she could barely get an interview.

I confronted one of my clients, an international strategic planning director, on this point directly. "Raymond," I said, "two years ago you would have hired Sandy Auerbach in a minute, now you won't even consider her. Is it because she's married to a competitor?"

I will never forget his answer.

"It's not that she's married to Tom Roman," he told me. "It's that she *acts* like she's married to him."

Tom, on the other hand, acted like nothing was any different. He tried to convince Sandy that this was best for him and consequently best for their family.

I heard recently that they're in marriage counseling. Sandy is still at home. Still out of work.

ALL PARTIES COULD HAVE WON

I have often wondered what might have happened, what might have been different, if there had been women on the board of directors of Sentry Industries. Had the board involved Tom and Sandy with the very real problem their relationship caused Sentry Industries, the very real brilliance of those two people might have found a solution that could have been fair and just and to the good of all the concerned parties.

But the board didn't know they could appeal to someone's values and safely share their company's vulnerability. And Sandy didn't realize that the game is played by people who subordinate individuals to rules and laws.

Had the board been able to use *relationalism* as a tool to solve a *situational* problem, they could have appealed to Sandy's reason and loyalty to Norman and Dearborn, and she may well have moved on and enjoyed the continuation of a powerful career. All parties could have won.

I often wonder where Sandy might be today had the board relied on the fine people involved rather than the fine print available.

Maria, Catherine, and Sandy: All committed Power Failure. All are still suffering, still not working, still stuck.

Vicki and Mary Louise: Both committed Power Failure.

Both did the challenging work of personal growth. Both are back on track, having transcended their crises.

And what of Amanda? Amanda provides a clear and thought-provoking example of a woman who committed Power Failure, suffered the fallout, and was able to learn and grow. In her courage and transcendence she is an example of both the pain and promise of this very real phenomenon.

Amanda

■

Why more was too much.

Several months after I had last spoken with Amanda Kitchen (in fact, several months after her baffling Power Failure), I was in Dallas and had dinner with Tony Fortuna, Amanda's first boss and mentor, who was doing a terrific job as executive creative director of J&L's Dallas office. He was bringing some New York savvy to their Texas operations. I had worked with Tony before—it was going to be good to see Tony again and catch up on his nearly two years as Dallas creative head. My real interest, however, was gaining insights into Amanda—and I thought Tony might be able to provide some.

"Tony, you must have been very excited about Amanda's Clio win. I didn't see you there that night—it was such a full house."

"I didn't go. I had too much work to do and couldn't be bothered with all that."

"Oh, that's too bad. It was a great evening. When was the last time you saw Amanda?"

He didn't answer my question and said instead, "You

know, BarBara, I know all about the B/B/L offer. I know how hard you tried to talk Amanda into taking that job."

Amanda had not revealed to me that she had consulted Tony. Surely *he* would have encouraged her to take this fantastic opportunity.

"It's exactly what she said she wanted—and more," I told him. "Amanda stated she wanted power to influence the industry. B/B/L offered her that power. I didn't know she had told you."

A small smile played across his face.

"Told me? She fuckin' came to me for advice."

"And you suggested . . ."

"I told her no one was offering *me* a press party." His eyes widened and seemed to double in size. "Or a seat on the planning committee. Or building me a goddamn nursery. And that *she* didn't deserve them yet. Not yet."

My mouth went dry. His anger and hostility were not something I would have anticipated. Where was it coming from? Why? When I found my voice, I tried a slightly different tactic. "Tony, do you think Amanda will ever realize her potential?"

"What do you mean?" he snapped.

"I mean, get on with her career, reach for the top."

He almost screamed it. "She's *at* the top now!"

Only in your narrow estimation, I thought to myself. "I don't see it that way."

"For God's sake, she's the highest paid woman at J&L," Tony concluded.

I had a rush of comprehension. Tony was, after all, her mentor. He was an executive creative director. Therefore, *she* could never be an executive creative director. That's what *he* was. She would be permitted to move a notch higher only if he did. First.

But Tony's chauvinistic attitude was not what made me feel both kicked in the stomach and relieved at finally understanding the truth. Or, I should say, the truth as felt—and acted upon—by Tony and Amanda.

I recalled Amanda's words from almost a year before: "No one ever beat Daddy."

APPRENTICES AND COMPANY WIVES

In some cases, the qualities that draw women very *near* the top may well be antithetical to those qualities that lead people *to* the top.

Specifically, relational values are expressed by many a career woman as unswerving loyalty, intense dedication to the goals of her group or department, or unflagging supportiveness of her boss.

Her work on *his* behalf actually furthers his career—and hers with it. Her willingness to champion his visions, to unhesitatingly give of her time and energy toward his stated goals, make her an invaluable employee. And she advances as he does.

In many ways, it is reminiscent of the highly valued "company wife." By pouring all her energies into her husband's endeavors, a woman enhances both his status and her own irreplaceability. Many women's driving efforts have enabled their husbands to graduate med school, win political seats, and achieve corporate power.

Tragically, if anything upsets that man's career, the woman's ambitions and status are also lost.

Today, many women further the careers of their mentors with the same vigor. And the same lack of self-focus. The only progress is, today they get paid for it.

Ideally, a mentor/student relationship is one of *temporary* inequality: The apprentice is to learn what the master knows and eventually assume full citizenship. Men generally approach this type of supportive learning arrangement with the goal of an eventual leave-taking. The attitude is: "I will further someone else's goals while I learn, then I will break off on my own." On the other side of the coin, a mentor usually knows that an ambitious individual who is learning is also performing. Care must be taken to give the best apprentices room to grow within the company, or they may well go to another company and become strong competitors. Thoughtful CEOs delegate legitimate authority to their lieutenants. Men expect this type of division of responsibility.

Women, however, as a group, have been in a position of *permanent* inequality in our society. They rarely approach a mentoring relationship with the goal of eventual independence and equality. (Equality with Father, for many women, is a scary place indeed.) Rather, they are still primed to achieve power by association. They focus their energies on two goals simultaneously: 1) the development of "his" career, and 2) the continuity of "their" relationship.

How is this different from the aforementioned "company wife" syndrome? In the external world of work and power, it is very different. In the internal world of relationships and perceived security, it may not be different at all.

A career woman who is supporting her mentor with her efforts is also achieving legitimate credentials for herself. She is developing her own résumé and references, if you will, which is very different from the situation of the supportive wife.

Emotionally, however, it may not feel very different at all. The disruption of the mentor/student relationship for any reason may leave the executive woman feeling adrift and without an anchor. Having never developed her own goals and visions, the loss of this important relationship may cause her to question the point of her working at all. She may perceive herself as directionless, and her working environment as devoid of the passion and energy she had previously experienced within it. She may suddenly perceive the workplace as a hostile and unfriendly arena where relationships are unstable and the continuity of connection is unlikely. In the wake of the disruption of the mentor/student relationship, she may respond by seeking safe and lasting connections elsewhere—by having children, focusing on her marriage, or devoting time to philanthropic groups.

RESPONDING TO A LOSS OF RELATIONSHIP

It seemed that Amanda had done exactly that—had a baby in response to losing her mentor.

After my dinner with an opinionated and surprisingly hostile Tony Fortuna, I reexamined what I knew about Amanda. I vividly recalled her telling me with a broad Texas grin, "No one ever beat Daddy." At the time it had struck me as a statement of both confidence and humility. After talking to Tony, however, it made me think that she had replaced the powerful Texas Daddy of her childhood with a powerful Texas mentor of her career life. Was Tony also someone in Amanda's internal world that "no one ever beat"?

I pieced together some other important facts: When I initially called Amanda about the B/B/L opportunity, she had been made a group creative director a year and a half before. She had taken Tony's job when he was promoted and transferred to Dallas. She told me her baby at home was six months old.

I did some quick calculating. Amanda must have gotten pregnant within three months of Tony's departure.

I have known lots of women who have gotten pregnant to effectively end their careers, or who used pregnancy to deal with a confusing or unrewarding career plateau or situation.

It turned out that Amanda "I-abhor-women-in-the-kitchen-commercials" Kitchen had become one of them.

■ ■ ■

A SENSE OF SEPARATE POWER

In contrast, a man whose mentor has left for whatever reason (e.g., retirement, transfer, death, promotion) is often empowered by the change. "This is my chance," he may think. Finally, he has the opportunity to achieve the ultimate goal of the original arrangement—he will take his boss's position. Men often feel the loss of the original relationship as a loss, to be sure, *and* as a challenge. "Now I can do things my way, move up, move forward." His sense of his separate power and individual vision is reinforced by the termination of this apprenticeship.

THE SUFFERING OF SAINTS

Consider the rise and fall of one of our most visible executive women, who disclosed her own inner motives: Mary Cunningham. In *Powerplay,* the autobiographical account of her intense but short-lived career at Bendix, she describes her feelings toward her boss and mentor, CEO William Agee, in almost religious terms. Her mission was to support and protect Agee, and she compares her plight to the suffering of saints.

October 9, 1988 was the eighth anniversary of Cunningham's resignation from Bendix. She told a *Chicago Tribune* reporter,

> I get calls in the middle of the night sometimes from women I've never met who are going through the same situation. I always talk to them and try to give them advice.

Cunningham said that one of her errors "was not drawing the line on how long the mentor experience would be." She told the *Tribune* that she recommends only a year. "For heaven's sake, limit the time you're under the auspices of one person."

Today, Mary Cunningham has just moved to Boise, Idaho, because her husband, former mentor Bill Agee, recently joined Morrison Knudsen Corporation as Chairman and CEO. Cunningham herself has eschewed the corporate world in favor of the Nurturing Network, which she founded and directs. Her network helps single pregnant women continue their studies and careers.

A POWERFUL MOTIVATOR

In assessing why a relationship with a mentor might *feel* so powerful and so essential for women, we again arrive at women's deep-seated relationalism. Consider this description from Jean Baker Miller's *Toward a New Psychology of Women:*

> [The women] all expressed a common theme: the lack of ability to really value and credit their own thoughts, feelings, and actions. It is as if they have lost a full sense of satisfaction in the use of themselves and all of their own resources—or rather, never had the full right to do so in the first place. As [one woman] put it, there is the sense that "there has to be that other person there."

As Miller continues, it seems striking how a close mentor relationship could be a powerful motivator for women:

> Unless there is another person present, the entire event—the thought, the feeling, the accomplishment, or whatever it may be—lacks pleasure and significance. . . . It is like being no person at all—at

least no person that matters. As soon as she can
believe she is using herself with someone else and
for someone else, her own self moves into action
and seems satisfying and worthwhile.

When we connect this internal view with the external reality
of executive women and their mentors, we begin to see a
powerful dynamic at work.

Morrison, White, and Van Velsor cite five major success
factors in evidence with their sample of seventy-six near-the-
top executive women. At the top of this list was "help from
above." In fact, of the five factors:

Every single one of the success cases in our study of
executive women was said to have had some help
from above. This is the only point in the entire
study on which all of our savvy insiders agreed!

LOSS AS CONSEQUENCE

The consequences of relationalism and power by association
can be many. In Amanda's case, the consequences were
losses—many losses.

She lost her sense of mission and purpose with her work.
She lost her power and reach. She lost the respect of management at J&L.

The human resource director at J&L in whom Amanda had
confided (and trusted) had honored Amanda's confidence by
running right to management and informing them of
Amanda's alternate offer. It had been foolish for her to confide
in him and in Tony—both Jones & Livingston career loyalists,
each with his own need and vested interest in keeping her in
place, keeping her *in* her place.

Because management would never again take her seriously

after she refused the position at B/B/L in Los Angeles, they kept her job focused on short-term results—good for them, not for her. To a man—and they were *all* men—not one of them would have turned down the job in her place. Not one.

She had also lost Ted. Just a few months after Amanda turned down the B/B/L job, Ted moved to Los Angeles anyway. I wondered what crises must have transpired between them in the wake of her Power Failure. Clearly, the balance and mutual respect that *had* existed in their marriage had been fiercely rocked.

There was a sociocultural loss as well. For all the women struggling to make ends meet, to cope with career and family—or, all too often, with dull, dead-end jobs and family— Amanda's unique arrangement could have made a statement and opened some doors. B/B/L and Amanda Kitchen could have turned her workplace into something closer to a Lifeplace. Her capacity to integrate the important components of *all* of her life could have been a blueprint for our still genderdivided culture. But Amanda was not ready to lead in this way, because she herself was not yet integrated. She didn't then have a handle on her own internal emotional forces, nor was she a woman who owned her own power.

I hoped Amanda would grow from her crisis, and have another chance. For herself. For her family. For all of us.

OVERCOMING POWER FAILURE

Amanda eventually did grow from this crisis, and was able to piece a life together based on her *own* power, not the power by association of her relationalism.

To do so, she had to follow a timeworn path of growth and change. There are four stages of work that are done by any woman who successfully overcomes or avoids Power Failure. They are:

1. Recognition of the problem
2. Acceptance of responsibility for solving the problem
3. Discovery of the genesis—the root—of the problem
4. Transcendence: owning one's own power

Amanda Kitchen eventually had to work through each of these stages. She is one of the courageous ones, willing to face her own emotional dragons even before she knows what they are.

QUESTIONS

Amanda called me at home late one night, nearly a year after the B/B/L opportunity.

"BarBara, it's Amanda Kitchen. I'll be in Chicago the next few days, judging the Addys. Can we get together for a talk?"

"Amanda, I'd love to see you. I hope to do more listening than talking, but I've got a few questions for you."

She laughed. "I've been living with a lot of questions of my own. Questions for which I haven't found answers. A few more questions can't hurt." Amanda had sounded bright and upbeat over the telephone, so I was surprised by her appearance as she entered Ciel Bleu for breakfast. She wore loose, dark clothing. She had gained weight. Her hair was pulled back in a reverse braid that suggested nothing beyond a serviceable style. She looked tired. As she shook my hand, she held my gaze for an extra long moment. This was not to be a casual breakfast. This meeting *mattered* to her.

"It's been about a year since I've seen you," I started neutrally.

"A *year,*" she said, sighing. "Yes, I guess it has been that long. Lindsay's walking and talking now."

"What else has changed?" I asked.

"Ted's gone, for starters." She searched my face to see if I had known.

I nodded and said I had heard that.

"Fast track, fun-loving couple on the fritz—yes, that's the kind of news people love to spread. It seems I'm still quite the role model, though."

I asked her to elaborate.

"My secretary told me the other day that I'm the role model of many of the new women in the agency. They find me successful and my life enviable and want to know what the magic shortcuts are so that they can 'be like me.' "

"And how do you see it, Amanda?"

"Like my life *was* enviable, *was* successful, but that's all been taken away somehow."

RECOGNIZING THE PROBLEM

I wanted to present my next idea carefully. Amanda had definitely taken the first step—she had recognized that a problem or many problems existed. Asking me to breakfast was a sign of that recognition, as was her honest expression of her feelings about her life.

The next step would be for her to take responsibility for the state of her own life.

"It's been my experience, Amanda, that it's not *taken* away as much as it's *given* away."

She looked at me hard for a minute, then said in a rush, "But BarBara, I don't think I could do any more than I already am. I work a full day every day, trouble-shooting without even a full group for support. Every night I play with Lindsay, and coordinate errands and shopping with Corazon. After we put Lindsay to bed, I watch an hour of prime time and an hour of daytime that I've taped, so I know what commercials are playing. I read *Ad Age* for a bit and go to bed. Mondays, Wednesdays, and Fridays I go to aerobics in the morning and Thursday after work I chair a women's advertising committee meeting."

"Doesn't sound like there's any time for rest or reflection," I commented.

"Well, Sundays I either call Ted in L.A. or sometimes he's back in New York for the weekend and we're a family again. Oh, yeah, and Sunday nights I always call my folks to tell them I'm surviving."

Her last statement sounded bitter, and she still didn't seem to be taking any personal responsibility. I decided to try again.

"It sounds to me, Amanda, like you've had a helluva year."

"I have."

"And that you've dealt with it by putting more stuff on your plate rather than more substance in your life."

"I should have taken that job, BarBara," she responded suddenly.

ACCEPTING RESPONSIBILITY

This sounded like a step toward taking responsibility for the problem. I prompted her to continue.

"I feel directionless at work. I'm very well paid, and they say 'a bit of a legend,' but I don't have my own group or my old clients. There's no partnership to develop strategies and goals. How the hell can I foster teamwork and commitment when there's no team to commit? They think they have placated me by calling me a trouble-shooter. Do you know what that really means? When some other group has run out of ideas or can't get anything past a client, they call me in 'to save the day.' And if I do? There are thanks all around and then that's it. 'Thanks. Now go back to your office.' I spend a lot of time in my office, BarBara, alone. I try to develop creative solutions for brands I don't have enough information on, for clients I've never met, where there's no history. And I don't have a team for input and perspective and energy. Worst of all, I don't get to present the work to the clients—I'm like the bastard child who's hidden from view. Without a champion, you know how quickly and efficiently your work can be destroyed."

I wondered if it was a champion or a mentor that Amanda missed at work. And anyone who was yearning for a champion wasn't yet taking responsibility.

"Did you used to have a champion, Amanda?" I asked her.

"If I'm in a meeting, I'll champion my own work. And Tony Fortuna used to support my work, too. He was a great boss." She paused. "Before . . ."

"Before?"

"Before he moved back to Dallas. And before I *didn't* move to L.A."

There it was, both events clearly on her mind, and back to back—Tony's moving away and her *not* moving forward.

"Are they connected in any way?"

"No, of course not." She looked shocked. "I mean, Tony was only a phone call away. We're real close friends—I even talked to him about B/B/L."

"And he said . . ."

"That I should definitely take any job I'm ready for."

An interesting and slanted paraphrase of what Tony must have said to her. His angry words to *me* had been: "She didn't deserve them yet. Not yet."

I asked her, "And weren't you ready?"

"I still haven't figured out the whole thing. For a few months, I was comfortable that I had turned it down. Until Ted left. Then I got confused about everything all over again."

"What happened with you and Ted?"

"Actually, BarBara, I believe the problems with us started *before* that incident. After Tony left, I started, oh, I don't know, turning to Ted for advice. I cried on his shoulder more. I just felt uncertain about everything. Then I was home for a month, and then half days. Ted still seemed very involved in everything that was going on at work. You know, J&L had even won a new account that I didn't even know they were pitching. That's how isolated I had been getting."

"How does this relate to you and Ted?"

"Well, with the B/B/L opoportunity, I started to see a way to get fired up again. Ted and I got very excited together. He even said he felt 'the old Amanda was back.'"

"What happened?"

"The closer we got to it, the more I was *sure* it was the best thing to do. Then I was sure it was the *absolutely wrong* thing to do. It seemed too frightening or something."

"How do you feel about it now?"

She straightened in her chair, and her voice became very firm.

"As if for the last two and a half years I've hardly been myself. I sold warm, confident commercials. Ted married a confident lady. Lindsay deserves a confident mother. I guess I'm having breakfast with you because I need to get that back."

I leaned back in my chair. She was accepting responsibility for her own part in turning down a fabulous opportunity and turning away a supportive husband.

Amanda reached over and took my hand, an unusual gesture for her, but not under the circumstances.

"BarBara, I feel like one of the walking wounded. This has been the worst year of my life. I won't take another one like it."

■   ■   ■

DISCOVERING THE GENESIS

There was a long pause while the two of us collected our thoughts.

I sensed that she wanted me to help her. I wanted her to help herself.

"How did you feel, Amanda, a year ago, when you turned that job down?"

"Confused. Relieved. Not as frightened as I had been."

"Frightened? What were you frightened about?"

"Success." She was playing for keeps, and she knew it.

"But you deserved to succeed. You had earned that."

"That has nothing to do with it, BarBara. If you succeed, it can mean only that someone else . . . has . . . well, failed." She quickly put her hand to her mouth. Her eyes filled with tears and there was a muffled, but distinct "Oh, my God" through her fingers.

Her shoulders suddenly relaxed. She lowered her hand from her mouth to the table where she moved her coffee cup aside. She turned back to me and said, with the greatest difficulty, "I can't talk for a minute."

And she didn't. Neither one of us did.

Then Amanda said, "Remember once, when I told you about my father?"

"I remember you told me, 'No one ever beat Daddy.' "

At this point Amanda recounted the skeet-shooting contest: the one she won. The one her father lost. The one that forever altered their relationship. The one that ended with Amanda's father telling her, "Kiss your trophy."

Amanda paused a moment to regain her composure, which she may have been on the verge of losing.

Amanda's insights into her childhood were a step toward discovering the genesis of her relationalism.

It had been quite a breakfast.

■ ■ ■

TRANSCENDENCE: OWNING ONE'S OWN POWER

In *Power Failure,* I've presented examples of six women who turned down powerful positions and suffered the fallout of their decisions. All had the opportunity to grow from this crisis, because it had hit them hard.

Amanda, Vicki, and Mary Louise saw it through all the stages.

Vicki recognized there was a problem immediately after Brian took the job in Boston. She then broke a family pattern by not following him, while preserving a family pattern by running for five years. During those years she accepted responsibility for her part in her career *and* her relationships. She looked deeply into her childhood, and sorted out the dual-role-model messages she had gotten from her mother. She returned to the States and finished her business with Brian and with herself. Finally a woman who owned her own power, Vicki again sought corporate power.

Mary Louise also made it through the necessary stages of growth. She had swung like a pendulum from being the in control, "total career woman" in her first marriage to being a compliant "wife" in her second. After many years of searching for the "expected" role to play, she started facing that there was a problem, and that it was hers to solve. In reaching a self-definition, she had much experience to draw upon—she had tried both the powerful and powerless roles she believed the culture had to offer. She struggled to understand the inequities buried in her own comfortable middle class upbringing, and the cultural and media messages she had taken to heart. In the end, Mary Louise was able to transcend her roles and become herself. At that time, she once again sought power, confident in her ability to lead, to set policy.

Like these two women, Amanda saw the process all the way through. She also did it in the shortest amount of time. And although certain opportunities, like the B/B/L position, are one-time chances, Amanda is still young, and has many opportunities ahead of her.

What of the others? Where did they get stuck?

Catherine recognized there was a problem. Her publicly collusive, unequal relationship (blustery Warren with his go-nowhere endeavors and an office at Catherine's company), and eventual divorce, her runaway son, her hospitalization, her firing—all these pointed to deep problems. And Catherine was aware of them all. I also believe she accepted responsibility for solving them herself. "I see now that Warren wasn't my whole life," she told me. "I built my career and I screwed it up and I can put it back together."

Somewhere after that, the process broke down. Perhaps she didn't do enough digging into her own relationalism. Perhaps she didn't see she was repeating a pattern with Zeke, but in an altered form. Somewhere Catherine got stuck.

Maria, whose life included only all-or-nothing choices, and Sandy, whose life seemed to be so full, with career and children and powerful husband, shared a similar lack of knowing. Neither one of them recognized the problem for what it was, and neither accepted responsibility for solving her own Power Failure, or even acknowledging her own role in it.

Maria seemed never to get beyond her father's litany of not quite belonging and that nothing but the "best" company could ever be good enough. She never cleared away these messages to look afresh at the real situation of her chosen field.

Neither did Sandy choose to acknowledge the problem, although people had been trying to get her to see it. Although she knew quite a lot about her childhood messages, she never seemed to relate them to her own loss of career or power. To this day she believes she was betrayed by "a man." A man to whom she is still married. Possibly, she is fearful that looking at her own actions might cause her to realize the price she paid for putting undying loyalty and blind relationalism over situational reality.

A lack of recognition of the problem and acceptance of responsibility for solving it means the crisis of Power Failure is not worked through. In the real world, the results of the lack of personal growth are clear: Catherine, Maria, and Sandy do not work at all, in any professional capacity, and the message they left our corporate culture is that women are not serious players. Vicki, Mary Louise, and Amanda all hold important managerial positions and are bringing their values to the corporate world.

AMANDA TODAY

Today Amanda is a different woman. Her revelation was the catalyst that freed her to succeed without the insidious and foreboding fear of the pain that success might inflict on the participants.

She knows what she wants.

She gets what she wants.

She wanted Ted back in her life and told him so. Ted realized very quickly that this was the "partner" to whom he had first been attracted. He said L.A. without her was just that—L.A. *without* her.

Ted's few months in L.A. had given him a valuable credential, and he considered returning to New York.

Some months later he did return to New York, to open a direct mail subsidiary of his L.A. agency. When he travels to L.A., he often takes Lindsay with him.

Amanda left Jones & Livingston—she had to break the pattern—and is now the executive creative director at Morrow Kline & Hewitt, where she personally handles the two best accounts in the agency and is in line for the presidency.

She has something else she didn't have before—her own power.

THE VISION OF LIFEPLACE

■

W E'VE SEEN that Power Failure is real. It exists now.
Women who state they desire power, who actively seek it, and
are offered it, will often, even then, turn it down.

It is happening with thousands of women in our corporations and professions. Frequently, it baffles and confuses corporate leaders, business writers, and equal-opportunity
advocates. At the same time, most women feel a familiar ring
when learning of other women who are torn between wholeheartedly embracing either career or fulfillment through others.

Fallout from this widespread crisis of self-definition is occurring everywhere. Women are not making it to the top. They
are not achieving top management posts in nearly the numbers
headily anticipated a decade ago.

Women both commit Power Failure and suffer Power Failure. While each of us individually has the power to create our
own lives and guiding principles, it is sane and appropriate to
accept where we have come from; the culture we've inherited
and the messages therein which still speak to us.

This culture has been polarized and compartmentalized. Rigid role and personality divisions have existed solely along gender lines. Love versus work. Home versus workplace. Each gender ethos was based on sacrifice of the other half of human personality. Men's lives were to be fulfilled by rational, objective, situational reality. Theirs was the grit of war, competition, rules, and the harsh conditions of the "real world." Women's lives, the ideology went, were to be drawn from these men and their children. Women's energy was to be applied to fostering development and confidence in those who had the outside world to reckon with. Theirs was the stuff of empathy, vulnerability, support, and the unending meeting of the needs of others.

These are the daughters and sons of industrialization and patriarchy. These are the Americans who have experienced a war every generation this century until the present one, and who structured corporations along military models. The same people to whom "Father Knows Best" and "Leave It to Beaver" were blueprints.

POWER FAILURE AND THE BRAIN DRAIN

Against this backdrop, the current state of affairs is a decided improvement over the past. No educated woman need depend upon a man for her economic support, nor fear for her survival in the event of death or divorce. Unlike Depression-era women, there are no state or local laws barring married women from gainful employment. Unlike women in the forties, today's women are not sent home to make room for returning soldiers. In contrast to the fifties and sixties, women today cannot legally be fired when they get married or are pregnant. Employment cannot be refused on the basis of sex, marital status, or family size.

In fact, the pendulum of equal opportunity has swung so far

that corporations actively court women for their management ranks. Discrimination, both overt and subtle, still exists to be sure, but there are many open doors.

Yet women still get exhausted and confused in the midst of a work culture alien to their guiding values and decision-making priorities. They still don't own their own power, and thus forfeit policy-making power.

While often capable of being situational and objective about their work, women's psychology causes them to operate personally out of a deep relationism. Because power by association is no longer necessary given the realities of the existing technological world, choices made on an outmoded model have the potential to wreak havoc in individual lives. Consider the losses, personal and professional, suffered by Maria, Vicki, Mary Louise, Catherine, Sandy, and Amanda.

A life driven by relationalism often catches up with the owner somewhere along the line, demanding final resolution of issues of separateness, selfhood and personal power.

Men's lives, situationally driven, also catch up with their owners, demanding a respect for integration, vulnerability, interdependence, and intimacy. Yet by the time—often, midlife and beyond—that men are seeking the other half of human values, men in the aggregate have obtained real world power.

Meanwhile, corporations are in the throes of the brain drain. Corporate leaders are starting to believe that women are productive, dedicated workers—who usually don't go the distance. Hire them into training programs alongside the men, and you have aggressive, talented executives of both sexes. For a while. Women don't seem to end up in leadership posts. The years and dollars behind women's training will produce an occasional powerhouse, but by and large the investment shows a startlingly different return compared to that in the young men. Get a woman near the top, the story goes, and she's likely to stop short! It's not even that she leaves for the competition, in which case the game seems fair. No, she's likely to leave for home or for self-employment. She might refuse to relocate. Or she may keep working, but the commitment seems to have vanished, replaced by a "putting in my time" malaise, or a bitterness coupled with a too-strict adherence to male norms; no personal vision seems to exist. Some men at the top are shocked and baffled, others rather expected it (and some of these helped it happen), and others ask, "What can we do to help them along?"

The answer, of course, lies only minimally with corporate leaders. The answers are within women themselves.

This is the state of Power Failure today. Where are we going? Before we chart a plan of action, it will be helpful to envision what might happen in the future as a result of decisions made today.

A MOMENT OF CHOICE

Currently, we are at a crossroads. Large technological and economic upheavals are occurring at the same time that women have gained entrée into the world of economic and public authority. This is a critical moment of opportunity for us to participate in the formation of a rapidly changing world. To decide what we want our contributions to be, we must consider the consequences of traveling either road.

If we travel down the difficult road of leadership by confronting the realities inside ourselves, our institutions, and our world, we will be instrumental in integrating the values of both genders into a currently polarized culture. The urgent issues of explosive technological change, the progress of equality and human rights, and child rearing appropriate for our times, need our full attention and participation.

If, instead, we take the path of least resistance, and retreat into familiar roles and expectations, we will burden the future with already outmoded models. The issues of gender equality and integrated leadership both beg for creative resolutions on personal as well as cultural levels. If we find them too painful to confront today, we will be living in a more complex and confusing tomorrow—and will still have them to face.

REGRESSION

Cultural change has lagged behind technological advances, and we are out of balance. Therefore, if we choose to regress, we will have all of today's problems compounded with all of tomorrow's.

What, actually, are we talking about? What do we stand to lose if we regress?

A lot.

A legal loss of equal opportunity, for starters. Many people do not think this could happen. "Granted, the ERA didn't pass," they will tell you, "but hundreds of laws at all levels of government guarantee equality."

Laws can be changed. Historically, the door of equal opportunity has snapped shut in times of crisis. For example, prior to child labor laws, children routinely stayed with the father in the event of a divorce. When children ceased to be a financial asset, and became, instead, a liability, "motherhood" was given separate status, and women were granted custody in most divorces—with little way to pay for their children's care and education. For another example, women were able to enjoy professional careers and public authority in the heady and prosperous 1920s. With the Depression, married women *lost their right* to gainful employment in many areas. Likewise, "Rosie the Riveter" made good money and helped win World War II. Business and government went to great lengths to encourage women's work—many initiated on-site day care centers. And closed them when they sent the "little women" home to make room for the returning men.

Even though equal opportunity is currently a legal right, we must not lose sight of the ephemeral nature of laws. The society creates laws that work for it. Equality is not yet an intrinsic right. It is still a privilege, because women are *not yet in policy-making posts* in widespread or representative numbers.

Consider these two hypothetical cases:

- A large corporation takes the EEOC to the Supreme Court with figures that show a huge percentage of their women executives leave the business world, compared with the men. In his concluding argument, the corporate counsel says, "To remain competitive with foreign companies, we must train not only our best minds, but *we must train people committed to remain productive employees.* Our records clearly show that women do not qualify."

- The business school of a prestigious university demonstrates that a significant percentage of their male graduates achieve top corporate positions, and a certain number become CEOs, COOs, presidents, and VPs. Their records also show that a huge percentage of female graduates *are no longer even in the corporate world,* and none have made CEO. They tell the court they have to reject thousands of promising male applicants each year to admit the women equally. They ask the court to okay an admissions policy biased on gender because they have sufficient indications that an applicant's *gender* is a factor in determining future success and public authority.

For each of these cases, the Court considers the Constitution, and the fact that it does not contain an amendment addressing sexual equality. The Court considers statistical tables, reviews the figures presented. It considers the corporation's need for hiring freedom sufficient to compete effectively in the world.

The Court—composed of eight men and one woman—decides.

Could women lose the equal opportunity they've gained?

Absolutely. The game in business is current and future value. The lack of passage of the ERA indicates the amount of conservative thinking that could be tapped in the event of widespread economic crisis.

On a less obvious but even more significant level than legal rights is the corporate perception of women as serious players. Already some corporate leaders are exhausted and unwilling to consider women further. In addition to the six stories told here, there are thousands of women in senior and middle management who are courted and aided, offered power, and turn it down.

At the corporations who have provided or offered childcare help, flexible hours, promotion without relocation, aid in relocating spouses, and other special benefits, only to watch their top management women "bail out," Freud's classic question haunts them: "What do women want?"

Regression at this time could also extract tremendous cost from the next generation.

To begin with, the group of women making the greatest strides toward equality are having the fewest children. Children raised by parents of equal power will still be a much smaller group than those raised in homes where polarization and gender roles are the rule. Even as this is being written, little boys and little girls are getting the message that women may work, but men have power.

Women will become autonomous and powerful in their lives, both at work and at home, by becoming powerful in themselves. Then they can translate this personal power into actions with others.

A further consequence of regression will be the lack of influence and participation by women in the future direction of our society and its guiding structures.

All of our current structures—the hierarchy of the corporate workplace, our Constitution and political systems, our legal and educational systems, even the need for a mobile nuclear family—were created by men.

In Alvin Toffler's view of the struggle between the Second Wave society we inherited and the emerging Third Wave:

> This sharpening super-struggle will decisively influence the politics of tomorrow and the very form of the new civilization. It is as a partisan in this super-struggle, aware or unwitting, that each of us plays a role. That role can be either destructive or creative.
>
> Some generations are born to create, others to maintain a civilization. The generations who launched the Second Wave of historic change were compelled, by force of circumstance, to be creators. The Montesquieus, Mills, and Madisons invented most of the political forms we still take for granted. Caught between two worlds, it was their destiny to create.

Toffler appeals to all of us to consider our actions carefully. Toward which ends are our efforts directed? Toward the past or the future? Do we take into account the realities of our times when adding our voices and our actions to the creation of new social organization? Toffler warns of possible consequences if we do not.

> [There is] the possibility of violence along the way to tomorrow. The transition from First Wave to Second Wave civilization was one long blood-drenched drama of wars, revolts, famines, forced migrations, coups d'état, and calamities. Today the stakes are much higher, the time shorter, the acceleration faster, the dangers even greater.

Power Failure occurs because massive cultural change has outstripped individual changes. The psyche of a nation has changed, but the psyche of the individual has not.

Power Failure exists not because women haven't changed, but *because they are not changing fast enough.*

In *The Third Sex,* McBroom offers this compelling reason why women's voices and values are so needed in the corporate world:

> Women . . . face in the workplace a culture created out of the masculine ethos with its own priorities, values, and unique history. That world bears the mark of a gender culture that is ignorant of and intolerant of most human needs other than achievement.

The need for compassion, ethics, and integration of gender values is extremely pressing in our corporations—because corporations have global impact, so many hours and years of our lives are spent in them, and, to quote *Corporate Cultures,*

> Corporations may be among the last institutions in America that can effectively take on the role of shaping values.

Let us not overlook that the vast majority of today's corporate leaders are men.

At this juncture of massive technologic, economic, and social upheaval and change, are we willing to again let only the "Montesquieus, Mills, and Madisons"—all men—develop the systems we all will live with?

We all will feel the tremendous cost of relationalism, of dependence, of traditional "femininity," if women's collective actions today result in the perpetuation of an unbalanced, skewed future societal structure, and add to the turmoil along the way.

Women have been struggling precisely because the current system doesn't work. As a society, would we regress into gender roles that would allow new forms to be created by only half the race?

BEYOND POWER FAILURE

Owing to the biological and technological realities that existed at the dawn of the industrial era, the current structure of the world of work and "real world" power was created in accordance with male values.

We are at a point of history where the old arrangements are decaying and the new ones are not yet conceived. Thus, it is a time of turmoil and uncertainty, both in our worlds and in ourselves.

It is time that women's voices and values be represented in the new forms of our culture. It is not a time when women need be victims, or need to find power by association.

How can women script the near future to keep regression at bay?

By owning their own power.

Today women have very appealing major problems to solve. The hope for the future lies within! By uncovering their relationalism and growing into powerful, integrated people, they will move into positions where they can affect policy.

It is possible for women to make the most of the current transitional moment, using the cultural crisis to move toward a vision of equality.

This will be difficult. There are no road maps, few role models. Many women will find themselves to be reluctant leaders.

By developing visions and values, and never losing sight of them, the tough choices become easier.

■   ■   ■

POWER BEGINS WITH THE INDIVIDUAL

The first step in obtaining corporate power is to develop personal power. Thus, the critical first changes must occur internally:

- From Maria to Amanda, these six executive women were *individually* offered power, and individually turned it down.
- Every crisis is a potential for growth. Women are on new emotional ground, and the challenge is to look inside oneself to meet the new social structures. To quote Carl Jung: "There is no coming to consciousness without pain."
- Power is a way of living; success is closure, termination of an attempt, attainment, already having.
- Power allows the implementation of one's own ideas and goals; the expression of an individual's unique voice in the world.

INTERIOR AWARENESS AND CHANGE

We have seen that men and women approach the world with psychologies that differ in significant respects. Men operate with a *situational* orientation, replete with rules and strategies and individual rights, while women rely on a *relational* orientation, based on mutual care and responsibility, trust, and connectedness.

In *The Third Sex,* McBroom tells us this about the internal conflict of women as they develop a professional identity:

There is a tendency to believe, in coming to this crossroads, that if a woman gives up her need to be good and altruistic, she will become bad and self-ish—as men are—or that if she stops being nice, she will become nasty. None of these things is true. The fears arise from prejudiced thinking about gender cultures. In becoming tough, women do not have to forfeit their kind, warm, and nurturant qualities, because these do not conflict with power and authority. Toughness and warmth are not opposites. What does conflict is the tendency to give power away, to put someone else in charge by serving, and altruistically to channel ego investments through men and children.

Women need to carefully view their gender psychology, and take a hard look at whether their internalized "truths" about relationships and feminine identity actually work for or against them in their careers and in their lives.

The following issues may serve as guides:

- Selfhood and separation. Women are often fooled by the *feeling* of security that relationalism holds: e.g., all the women in our stories acted relationally, and *all suffered net losses.*
- Internal, intuitive feelings of the "way things should be" may not be a guide to correct action. These may be based in *past* not *future* realities. Women need to mentally correlate their actions with their life values.
- Women don't need to discard their natures; rather, they need to incorporate them into a fuller reality; recast relationalism as a *tool,* as one of many choices of behavior, as an aid to establishing an empathetic leadership; realizing that actions based on relational-ism alone may not serve.
- Recognition of situations in which connected, affilia-tive behavior is appropriate versus those in which

rules, structure, and "the game" should be primarily attended to.

- All problems are solvable. It is critical for women to create innovative solutions that don't require a reduction in women's equality or input.
- Power Failure can be overcome or avoided by working through four growth stages:
  1. Recognition of the problem.
  2. Acceptance of responsibility for solving the problem.
  3. Discovery of the genesis—the roots—of the problem.
  4. Transcendence: owning one's own power.

WOMEN AND POWER IN THE CORPORATE WORLD

Women's lack of *internal power* is often in conflict with what is necessary in the *external reality* of the workplace. Having hoped that work would be fulfilling and liberating, modern women have rarely accepted the world of work for what it actually is.

Opportunities have outstripped consciousness.

Without real personal power, women have just shifted their labor from home to office, and by "bailing out," do not improve their situation, but trade it.

This is an exciting time we live in. Real-world options are available to women today—chances at power that were previously unavailable. Undeniably there are still problems—inside and outside women themselves. But problems can always be treated as opportunities for personal and societal growth. While the world of corporate power is largely uncharted territory for women, it is also an opportunity for creativity. It is an adventure.

To become more realistic about and personally committed to the world of corporate power and opportunity, women must carefully assess the world they have chosen to enter:

- Power begets policy. The game is determined by those in power: men. Women in power will be able to set policy differently, but first they need to obtain power.
- Technology allows choice. Requirements of work no longer presuppose divisions by sex.
- Women must not look to men or to organizations to provide them opportunity. Organizations don't make changes. People make changes, and changes redefine organizations.
- People are not "rewarded" for loyalty. Rather, they are hired (and paid accordingly) in expectation of the work they will be able to do, the problems they will be able to solve.
- Windows of opportunity exist where there are needs. Without problems there are no real opportunities.
- By placing their hopes in security and loyalty, women miss the point that the game in business is *current* and *future* value.
- Many corporate leaders are not inflexible or unresponsive to individual needs. People will make special compensations for special contributions; e.g. a nursery for Amanda Kitchen's daughter, an office for Catherine Ames's husband.
- Corporate power is possible only for those who are *self-empowered.*

▪ ▪ ▪

THE VISION OF LIFEPLACE

The separate arenas of home versus workplace and love versus work have divided our very selves. To erase these divisions and unify all the important tasks and values of our culture will require the collective energies of as many people as possible. It is our charge to create Lifeplace.

The polarization of the past developed a society based on war, domination, and sacrifice. Integration enables peace, independence, and community.

To move toward Lifeplace, women must first understand the root psychology of, and liberate themselves from, Power Failure.

Women's first steps toward power were, quite rightly, to launch a revolution. Revolutions start by blaming others, assuming oppression and injustice. The women's movement began this way, but the need for widespread revolution may have passed. Today there may be more effective strategies for creating changes in our institutions. Now women *do* have access to the world of business and public authority. Changes may be made from *within* the corridors of power. Today the need is for women to find their own voices, feel their own power, recognize it, own it, and express it.

The problems women currently face represent a noble and exciting struggle: The women's movement (now just twenty years old) has changed the nation's psyche, and the next step is to change the psyche of the individual. A balance of power at the top will give male and female leaders a solid opportunity to integrate values and styles to make the workplace a Lifeplace.

Women must look to themselves alone to forge a better vision, to lead, to be willing to be alone at the top, where no one is left above to lead the way or smooth the path, and everyone below looks for guidance.

To solve Power Failure, women must take an entirely new

look at the violated expectations they experience in the work-place. By viewing problems as opportunities to embrace, they can psychologically reposition solving life's harsh realities as a meaningful and exciting approach to modern existence—a journey that begins with and requires power.

In liberating themselves from an outmoded relational orientation, and thus solving Power Failure, women will be instrumental in integrating those parts of all our lives that have been segmented. Women in the future will insist that home and workplace be integrated into a Lifeplace, and our children will have even greater opportunities to participate fully in their world.

As women seek, obtain, and exercise power, it will be their charge—and their chance—to be self-empowered, to integrate gender values, to unite the separate arenas of love and work, home and workplace.

It is our view that women need to be at the top in positions of power so that their voices are among those drafting the new culture, creating Lifeplace.